PAY THE COST

MICHAEL BRANCH

Published by:

Legit Styles Publishing
16501 Shady Grove Rd., Suite 7562
Gaithersburg, Maryland 20898
www.legitstylespublishing.com

ACKNOWLEDGEMENT

First and foremost, thank God because without him none of this would be possible. Big shout out and thanks to the Legit Styles Publishing team and Byron "Ceo" Grey, for believing in my vision and bringing it into existence. I am here because I have been lifted onto the shoulders of many loving people from family to friends. I would not be here if it weren't for their love, attention, hearts and support. Boundless thanks to my son Dashawn Michael Branch for striving to achieve any and everything you have set your mind to do. Also, for accomplishing so many goals in life at such a young age. We all believe you are going to be someone special and important to this world. I love you son with all my heart, you are truly a blessing to me. Sending my love in hopes of reaching your hearts; my mom Karen Hall and Grandmother Shirley Hall. Two of the most beautiful women ever in my life. Please continue to watch over me from above. I miss you and love you dearly. To my dad, I love you man because you have always seemed to be there for me when it counts the most. To my little brother Lamar Porter, funny how you have grown into a man overnight. I love you for stepping up and holding the family down. Special thank you and appreciation to my little sister that acts as if she was my big sister. I love you for being the realest understanding, loving sister that has been beyond supportive to me. A true soldier that has shined so much light on this solitude I have had to deal with for the past 12 years. Sis you are my rock, my Navy Seal that seems to always pull me out when it seems like it is me against the world. To my two long distance brothers that had my back through thick and thin, days I will always remember and nights I will never forget. To Don "Big Head" and Terrance "Zay" Delly, I love you all for life. To my son's mother Tamerah "Mia" Lane for taking on the responsibility of being both parents and raising our child into the fine young man he is today. As a single mom, I feel you do not get the credit you rightfully deserve and I know these words are not enough but do know I very much appreciate you and you are the true definition of a super mom. To all my aunts and uncles, I love you all with all my heart. To all my cousins, I love you all, stay strong and always family first after God. A big tremendous shout-out to my business partner D-Deuce for always keeping it real and being a stand-up dude. They say God always gives his hardest battles to his strongest soldiers; you fit that description and wear it well. Solute to a real nigga. My last shoutouts goes to those who are locked down but never forgotten. Seagram, Geeze, Author Don Twan, Yak, Dave, Bree, Zay, Cheese, Fetty Mac, DP, Rico, Meech Face, words of wisdom for you all. God grant us the serenity to accept the things we cannot change, the courage to change the things we can and the wisdom to know the difference. Anything is possible when you got numbers.

CHAPTER ONE

Parked in a one level garage across the street from a strip club called Norman Jeans, Floss reclined in the driver's seat of his 2001 Mercedes. It was the brand new S500 series, with arctic white interior, cocaine white paint, and it sat on 22-inch Lexani rims. While relaxing with his eyes closed, he had one of his hands placed on the back of Candy's head, directing and controlling her every movement. The Benz was topped off with limo tint, giving complete privacy to him as he enjoyed the club's exclusive stripper. Candy expertly bathed his dick with the best head in the city, and her lips and tongue did tricks David Copperfield would've been proud of.

"Ssssss, damn!" he hissed, as his toes curled in his hightop Gucci shoes.

Candy looked up at him with sultry eyes. Gripping his member, she slapped it roughly against her jaw before putting it back into her wet mouth.

"Umm," she moaned as if the taste of him satisfied her.

Candy was mixed with Ecuadorian and Dominican, which gave her an exotic look, and made her stand out from the rest of the strippers. She was known for being one of the baddest bitches working in Norman Jeans, and she knew it.

Norman Jeans was a small strip club that sat in the middle of the block on Baltimore Street. The Elite club had Baltimore City's finest women, along with a mixture of women from New York, New Jersey, Philly, Delaware, DC, and Virginia. Floss could not resist Candy. As soon as he stepped into the club she approached him, and prevented any contact with other women unless she approved. Candy was very possessive when it came to him. Although she wasn't the type to express her feelings or show her emotions, Candy had to admit she was falling hard for Floss. One of Maryland's youngest ballers, who had the city of Pasadena on smash, and all the strippers knew it. And because of that, he enjoyed all the perks that came along with it. Candy slowed her strokes, as she felt him tense up.

"Ain't nothing like a bad bitch with some bomb head," he whispered as he opened his eyes and looked into hers.

Candy knew she had him hooked because Floss always told her how he loved looking into her natural, green eyes. He loved how she stared him down while she gave him head.

"You gonna swallow this, baby girl?"

"Is that what you want? Would you like that?" she asked, as her tongue played with the underside of his dick, sending a tingling sensation through his body.

"Here it comes!" Floss arched his hips, his dick went deeper into her throat, and just before he could reach his climax; he was woke from his vivid dream.

"Yo cellie!!! Aye Floss!!"

He opened his eyes.

"What!"

His cellie, Miles, stood over him as he laid on the bunk. "It's chow time. Are you eating?"

Floss grabbed his dick beneath the covers, while training his eyes to see. "Chow Man nah, I'm cool."

"Aight, I just wanted to make sure," Miles said, as he turned to leave the cell.

As Miles left, Floss exhaled a long sigh. The dream still held a grip on him as he struggled to gather his senses. While rubbing his eyes, he tossed the covers from his body, sat up, and placed his feet on the floor.

The cell that he was confined to was a 12 x 9 room, with two steal bunks, a sink with a toilet attached to it, and a small window that was broken. That pissed his cellie Miles off more than anything, because he needed fresh air to relax and sleep at night. The walls were painted off white, a little metal tan table was bolted to the concrete floor, and to top it off, a dull pocket size mirror that you could barely see your reflection in.

Floss shook his head, "Fuck, how did I get in this bitch?", he wondered, dropping his head in his hands. Many questions began running through his head. How he managed to get captured by the Fed's, and who in the hell was the Government's key witness against him. The more he thought about it the more his head began to ache. He got up and washed his face, looked at himself in the mirror, and pulled his long dreads into a ponytail. At twenty-two years old, his lawyer told him he was facing a lengthy sentence; something he never expected in a million years.

"Everybody line up for chow!" The CO's voice boomed throughout the unit.

Floss looked out of his cell door and saw that he still had time to get a tray, which was good because he was actually hungry as hell. He just hated that his cellie woke him up, especially during a dream about Candy. The event with Candy brought him back to all those the times he enjoyed busting nuts in her mouth. Now it seemed like many lifetime's ago, instead of only months.

7

Everything about the unit had a dull vibe. From the dull tan paint, to the outdated 27-inch TV that hung from the wall with only three channels. It had four tables, one hot pot, one computer, and four phones that were stuck to the wall. The unit was small so it made voices carry, and at times it was difficult to hear on the phone or watch TV. To make things worse, the spirits of angry men filled the air with tension. Most were waiting to receive a lengthy sentence from an unjust system, and everyone was torn away from their loved ones. The surroundings made Floss think long and hard about all his actions and now fate will show if he will pay the cost.

Putting on his Prada's, he stepped out of the cell. Cats were rushing to get in line like the food was going to run out. This was his first time being locked up and he was barely getting use used to the food. Dragging his feet, he made it up to the front of the line, watching the female CO as she waited to serve.

"Damn, baby thick huh?"

Floss looked at the young dude named Chill.

"Yea she's cool," he said.

He had to admit, the chick had an hourglass figure with a face out of this world. She was one of the few black women who worked there. But due to his situation, Floss didn't pay her very much attention. The line moved, and after getting his tray he found a seat at the table with Miles.

"I thought you was cool?"

"Man, I gotta eat something. I can't wait until commissary comes tomorrow." Looking at the mashed potatoes, mixed vegetables, and mystery meat swimming in dark liquid that was supposed to be gravy; his stomach turned.

"Shit, me too," Miles laughed.

Floss was being held in Talbert County Jail, located in Eastern Shore Maryland, while he waited to be transported to county. His unit was filled with dudes who committed various crimes, from white collar shit to bank robberies. Only a few of them had drug cases and his cellie was one of them.

"I can't finish this shit," Floss said shaking his head. Up to that point, he was picking over his food like a kid does with vegetables.

"Aye man let me get it," a guy named Mikey said.

People called him Mikey because he would eat anything. Floss slid his tray to him, got up, and made his way over to the phones. He figured he would call his baby mamma Tia, to see if she handled what he asked her to. After a few rings she answered and accepted the call.

"Hello."

"Hey," she said. Her voice sounded tired.

"What's going on?"

She sighed. "Nothing, Da-Da started preschool today. He asked when you were coming home."

Floss hated being away from his little man. He was his one and only, and to not be there for his first day of school was punishment in itself.

"Tell him daddy will be home soon. Did you talk to Mr. Ravenell?"

Kent Ravenell was his new lawyer and because of the bullshit he went through with his old one, he kept Tia on his ass.

"Yes. He told me he's putting that in the mail to you today, "she replied.

Since he was told he had a confidential informant testifying against him at his trial, Floss asked his lawyer to send him the name. He was dying to know who they had, because not knowing was stressing him out. He kept his circle pretty small, so he was confident that whoever it was, could not be a person who really knew his business. That was his only hope, in order to beat the conspiracy charges against him.

After hearing Mr Ravenell sent him the information, he needed to fight his case, Floss and Tia spent some time talking about their relationship. He felt fucked up about being locked up and depending on her, especially after all the shit he took her through.

Floss was sure to let Tia know how much he appreciated her, and when this ordeal was over, he promised to make it right by her.

"Just do right by your son, I'll be alright," she said.

So many things ran through his mind that he wanted to say. But he didn't want to go into detail about how he was going to change once this was over. He told her that many times before. And on each occasion, Tia simply expressed how she would believe it when she saw it. So instead, Floss asked her to bring their son to visit that weekend.

"We'll be there, do you need any money?" she asked.

"Nah, I'm still good," he told her. Noticing his cellie waving to him, Floss told Tia he would call her back.

"Okay. But wait until tomorrow when your mom brings Da-Da back. I'm tired so I'mma get some rest."

"Alright then, I love you."

Tia was silent for a moment, before she responded. "I know and I love you too."

Hanging up, Floss went over to see what his cellie wanted. He was standing near the slider that divided their unit from the one next door. Floss knew that nine times out of ten there was a message for him.

"Ayo, Boodah's callin for you," Miles told him.

Stepping to the slider, Floss knocked twice.

"Yo! Floss!"

"Yea, what's up?" he asked recognizing Boodah's voice.

"Did your lawyer shoot that yet?"

Although Boodah couldn't see him, he shook his head. "Hell nah, yo. The only mail I got was from my bitch."

Since he was transferred to Talbert County, he and Boodah had grown close. At one time they were at odds on the streets; two young hustlers beefing behind a misunderstanding. But now the two of them were being snitched on, and with Boodah's advice, Floss requested the information from his lawyer to see who was telling.

"Well," Boodah began, "My lawyer sent me the names of the niggas rattin on my shit."

"Oh yeah!" This was good news to Floss.

"Yeah, and a few are from the city."

Floss tensed.

"Ayo, you tryna' check it out?" Boodah asked him.

"Hell yeah!" Floss wanted to see if he knew any of them.

The sound of paper rattling came as an envelope slid beneath the door. Bending, Floss picked it up. "Okay I got it."

"Just shoot it back when you done. Man, Floss we gotta make sure these bitch niggas don't show up to court. Cuz if they do, these cracka's gon' try to put us away for life. So, look and see if you know any of them niggas." Boodah's tone was dead serious.

"Fo'sho."

Floss stepped away from the slider and headed straight to the cell. Miles was on his heels, just as interested to know the names of the informants listed on the paper. Once the two were inside the cell, Miles pulled the door shut, as Floss took a seat on the bunk. Anticipation gripped Floss as he unfolded the paper. There were several pages, so he shuffled through them, as his eyes scanned the page with names underlined in blue ink.

Miles stood over him looking down. "Damn how many names are there?"

He shook his head. "Man, this nigga Boodah got all kinds of dudes tellin' on him."

"Do you recognize any of 'em?"

Floss slowly shook his head, continuing to look. As he examined each name, he realized how many cats he knew only by their nicknames, not their government. But that didn't stop him. He took his time reading over each, and some were even women.

Miles was anxious. "All them rat ass niggas!" he spat in frustration. "We need to shoot that shit to the streets, so niggas can hunt them down."

Hearing his cellie, Floss tried to concentrate. He was growing frustrated himself as he saw all the people telling on Boodah. At first the man had no idea who was snitching on him, but now he was sure.

"Fuck, yo! I don't see anybody on here I know. It only has niggas governments on here." Floss said growing agitated.

"Here, let me check it out."

Floss handed the papers to his cellie and instantly felt a migraine coming on. Laying back on his bunk he closed his eyes and could not stop his mind from wandering. *Who is telling on me? Out of all the niggas I helped get money!*

Miles began making comments, cursing and talking about how snitching was becoming common. But Floss only heard it in muffled tones. All he thought about was the mandatory twenty years his lawyer told him he was facing, and how he only sought to provide for his mother, little brother, and sister. He was trying to be a man, while his father sat in a cell just like the one, he was now in.

"Man, you need to try and think about who the fuck is tryna' hit the stand on you Floss!"

Opening his eyes, he looked at his cellie.

"Real shit yo," Miles told him. "Cuz if you can't kill they ass first, then these people are gonna hide you until you old and gray; maybe 'til you dead."

Floss let the words his cellie spoke sink in deep. The reality of his situation hit home as he laid there. He knew right then and there that he only had one option: find and kill the informant on his case. But first he had to identify him. Floss didn't know who to start with, so he began at the beginning of it all; from the first day he got into the game.

1996

Back in the Dayz

CHAPTER TWO

J ust outside the city of Baltimore, Maryland, is another city called Annapolis. Known by many for its naval and shipping yard, Annapolis would rock a stranger to sleep. Many crime infested neighborhoods existed in the city and one was just miles away in Pasadena, Maryland, called Freetown. A place where drugs, violence, and other illegal activities occurred, twenty-four hours a day; seven days a week.

This was Floss' home, the hood he represented, running with the best of them. With his father in prison and his mother struggling to raise him and his younger siblings, he did everything in his power to be the man he needed to be.

Freetown sat tucked away from the main streets of Ritchie Highway, and Mountain Road; three sides of the neighborhood was surrounded by woods. Old Freetown Road was now New Freetown Road, it curved through the neighborhood filled with old, red, brownstone town homes; with two, three, and four bedrooms. Freetown was a total of six buildings with three stories each: three buildings at the top of the complex, and three at the bottom. The top of the housing project was called Levy Court and the bottom was called Shirley Murphy Court. A trail that led through the woods gave Floss easy access to the residential and the project side of Freetown. Each day he would wake up, jump on his BMX bike, and make his way to the hood to see what he could get into.

It was a little past 5:00 p.m. and the block was jumping. Cats were out hustling and sitting on brand new whips enjoying the fast money crackheads spent. Floss rolled up the street looking for his road dog, T-Roy.

"Whassup little nigga?"

Floss looked at his big homie Fat Cat who was posted up with a few older dudes from the hood.

"Whassup?" he hollered back, sending head nods to Fat Cat and the others. He had major respect for them and loved how they got money.

Shirley Murphy Court was located at the bottom end of New Freetown Road. This was where Floss headed to, looking for T-Roy: he found his partner standing out in the courtyard serving a fiend. With only two years separating them, T-Roy was the elder, so he was a little advanced on his grind.

"Ayo, what's up Floss? Damn, my nigga where the fuck did you go?" He parked the bike by a friend's porch and walked over to T-Roy.

"I had Monique braid my hair and went home to take a shower." His freshly twisted cornrows were pulled tight and greased.

T-Roy pulled a small knot out of his pocket. "I made almost two hundred already. But Fat Cat and them up front getting all the money."

"That's cool. They can't get it all."

"How much work you got?"

Floss pulled out the few rocks he had in a plastic bag. "Like four twenties."

"Well, let's walk up to Levy Court. I know it's some money up there."

As they were making their way to Levy Court, they noticed an unfamiliar black Crown Victoria turn down Old Freetown Road, doing about sixty mph.

"Man, whos...."

Right as T-Roy was about to make a comment, Floss noticed that the car was filled with dudes from their rival neighborhood, Pioneer City. Then, speeding to a screeching halt the doors to the car flew open, catching Fat Cat and the others off guard.

Pop....Pop...Pop...
Boom...Boom...Boom....
Pop.... Pop...Pop...
Boom...Boom...Boom....

The sound of gunfire erupted, sending hustlers, dope fiends, crackheads and innocent bystanders scrambling for cover.

"Oh shit!" Floss yelled, as he and T-Roy darted between an old Ford pickup truck and Honda Accord.

The gunfire continued for a few more rounds before ending abruptly. Floss and T-Roy were huddled between the two vehicles, listening as the screech of tires echoed down the street. Figuring it was over, they came out to see if the coast was clear.

"Come on, let's go see if anyone got hit," T-Roy told him.

Floss followed his homeboy up the street. No one got injured which was a miracle. It was confirmed that the cats from Pioneer City were behind it, because of a club fight the two neighborhoods had the weekend before. Floss knew it was more than that because their beef originated years prior. He knew the shooting and brawls would probably continue forever.

One of his older homeboys named Dell was laughing. "Them bitch ass nigga's niggas ain't hit shit!"

Another older cat named Lump agreed. "Dumb ass niggas can't even shoot straight," he said, also laughing.

As Floss listened, he observed everyone being a little too relaxed with all their smiling faces and laughter. To him this was no laughing matter, and someone could have easily gotten killed. He saw his older homeboys consuming weed and alcohol, and he felt this was their downfall; they were slipping, never focused, never on point.

"What's so funny about ducking bullets?" he whispered to T-Roy.

His partner only gave him a look.

He continued. "Man, it's time we got a gun."

The fact that they didn't have one was a mistake, and Floss felt it would be safer to be caught with one than without.

T-Roy nodded. "Alright, I'll put the word out."

For the rest of the night, Floss asked himself if he was really ready for the game. His pops was a certified G from the streets, and his mother was a G as well. That night he promised himself if he was going to be in the game, then he was going to be different than the crowd he ran with. He would never take threats lightly and would keep his mind on what mattered most, the money.

T-Roy was getting his crack from an older cat from their hood named Los. Once they got the work, it was a race to see who could sell their packs the fastest. T-Roy was more advanced in the game and making more money than Floss. As a youngin', Floss saw a lot and recognized more; especially how Los fronted for all the youngsters in the hood, like he was tough shit. But just weeks prior, he saw Los get bitched by some cat from another hood, and he didn't even retaliate.

Floss took a mental note: Los was really a clown, and he just "acted" hard in the hood.

As for the contest, it was always between T-Roy, Rico Suave, Russ, Floss, and a few more hustlers their age. Whoever lost would end up paying for everyone's food for a week. In the end, Floss would have to pay for the food for a whole week which was the agreement.

One night on the block, a crackhead hopped out of an old Honda Accord, moving like he had a million dollars; the older cat hopped up the curb towards them.

"Hey youngin'," he said, with his eyes wide open higher than giraffe pussy.

Floss flew towards him with T-Roy on his heels. "What's good old-timer?"

"I got this thirty-eight revolver," he said pulling out a small black handgun. "I'm tryna' get an eight-ball for it."

Floss nudged his homeboy. "Man let's piece up and get it."

Agreeing that they needed a gun, the two huddled where the smoker couldn't see what they were doing. They quickly put a few twenty-dollar rocks in a plastic bag, went back to the fiend, and Floss let T-Roy do all the talking.

"And it's that fire shit!" T-Roy said, hyping up the product.

The man looked at the small bag of stones like he wanted to protest. However, his craving overrode all sensibility. "Alright but y'all owe me one."

When the man pulled off, the two friends started laughing. They got the shit out of dude.

"Let me check it out," Floss said.

When T-Roy handed Floss the pistol, something in it sent a surge through his body; like it gave him power. Gripping it in his hands, he knew right then and there if anyone threatened him, or his hood again, he was busting shots. Now singing Nas' song, I gave you power.

"How you like me now, I go POW it's that shit that moves the crowd, making every ghetto go foul......"

***

Floss' mother moved into the three bedrooms when he was ten years old. With two bedrooms upstairs and his room downstairs, he would come in and out whenever he pleased. Everyone called his mom Bell, and everyone had much respect for her. Although he remembered little of her hustling days, Floss heard many stories of how his mom and dad were like Bonnie and Clyde but getting money on the streets with the best of them.

Beep...Beep. ..Beep

The small Motorola pager went off, waking Floss from his deep sleep. When he rolled over, he realized it was late in the morning. Reaching, he grabbed the pager off the dresser and looked at the screen. 444 was the code him and T-Roy used for them to meet up at the spot. Jumping up, he washed his face, brushed his teeth, and shot out the house on his bike through the woods.

Pops was an older smoker who use to let them serve out his house. When Floss arrived Pops was gone, and T-Roy answered the door smiling from ear to ear.

"What's good my nigga?"

Floss tossed his bike to the side. "Nothing, what's good?"

When Floss stepped inside, T-Roy had two hood chicks sitting on the couch that he had never seen before. T-Roy was known for having a way with the chicks, and by their good looks, it seemed like something was up.

"This is my homeboy, Floss,." T-Roy introduced him.

Both girls smiled seductively. "Hey Floss," they said in unison.

Now Floss was far from a virgin, and it was nothing for him to toss a crackhead a rock and get some head. There were times him and T-Roy would pick up high school chicks at the Marley Station Mall and bring them back to Pop's spot. So he knew what time it was.

"Ok I see y'all shorty, what it do?"

T-Roy stood next to him and got straight to the point. "Which one you want?"

He looked at both girls, who were obviously older than him. Dressed in booty shorts and halter tops that accentuated their young breasts, Floss smiled.

"Shit...we can swop swap it out," he told his partner.

T-Roy patted him on his back, as they both looked at the seductive two. "Yeah sounds good to me."

For hours, they were held up in Pop's spot fucking on the two chicks, switching back and forth. Floss and T-Roy got their dicks sucked, and even had a competition to see which chick could ride dick the best. Even though he wasn't a virgin, he was still somewhat inexperienced, and one chick noticed quickly; she did things that later had him wide open.

"Damn yo," he said to T-Roy later that night on the block.

"Baby girl had that fire wet. I'm tryna' hit that again."

But T-Roy thought differently, "Man fuck dem hoes. It's M-O-B... Money over bitches. Never forget that, son."

Floss shook his head. "Shit, pussy and money feel the same to me. What's the difference?"

T-Roy laughed. "You got a lot to learn youngin." "Who me?" "Man, you got a lot to learn."

Floss was a little offended but by his partner's comment. "What's wrong with me saying they feel the same?"

Taking his time, T-Roy gave Floss his thoughts on the matter. He explained how pussy could make a man lose focus in the streets. Money could buy everything, but pussy could only get you killed or run you broke trying to chase it.

"If ya money right then the pussy will follow," he continued. "Pussy can only get you an STD young nigga."

Now it was Floss' turn to laugh. "Well if you know so much about bitches why you ain't a pimp?"

"That shit ain't for me! A pimp will do anything for money, even sell his own ass. That's why."

To Floss, it seemed T-Roy had an answer for everything. That's why he liked him. But he knew T-Roy's real reason for not trusting women came from his ex-girlfriend breaking his heart. It was his first love, so all his game about females rooted from that one experience. Her leaving him while he was in juvenile jail, left T-Roy bitter as hell.

Word in the hood was that Fat Cat, Dell and some more OG's retaliated for the shooting that occurred. A few cats from Pioneer City got hit, and two were left in critical condition. All the drama kept a lot of hustlers off the block, so T-Roy and Floss took advantage of it. They were selling packs fast and it was time to re-up.

"Ayo, I'mma' hit Los up. So, we can have some more work for the late night rush."

Floss knew they would need it, but something else was on his mind. "Hey, let me ask you a question."

"Go ahead. What's up lil homie?" T-Roy asked.

"What's with that nigga Los?" he wanted to ask him this for a while, but he knew his homeboy looked up to the nigga.

T-Roy said, "Man, ole' boy use to put in that work on these streets."

But Floss was not impressed. "Yeah, that's what they say."

"You don't sound convinced. See lil homie, the reason he ain't putting in work no more is because he got us. He's holding us down with these packs."

"Nah, he got you! All I'm doin' is fuckin' with you."

"But when he hooks me up I hit you off." T-Roy said. "It helps us both."

Floss shook his head. "To me dude is just fake. I mean, he's up in that big ass house while we're out here sellin' his shit. Do you think he really cares about you?"

Without hesitating T-Roy said, "Hell yeah. You too! We're his little homies."

saying another word, Floss made a mental note. He wanted to see if Los really gave a fuck about them and he needed a way to find out. That night he told himself he was going to find a way; all he needed was the right plan and some time.

CHAPTER THREE

Winter was coming and the weather was extra cold out. Floss was dressed in thermals under his Armani Exchange jeans, and Hermes' sweater, sporting a Northface jacket, and some Timberland boots. The block was really slow, and he and T-Roy were growing tired of hanging out.

T-Roy rubbed his hands together, blowing in them. "It's getting cold out here, so I'm going to call this shorty and see if she got a friend for you. I know all you think about is getting some ass, and I like to put a smile on my lil man's face."

Floss laughed.

"What's up? You down?"

He nodded. "Fuckin' right."

The two headed to Pop's spot to use the phone. When Pops answered the door he looked like he saw Santa Clause.

"Aye!! Come on in y'all," he said, smiling happily. Floss and T-Roy entered with Pops shutting the door.

"I'm glad to see yall. Somebody give me a bump til later on," Pops requested immediately.

"I got 'chu," T-Roy said removing a small pebble sized rock from his crack sack.

With the quickness, Pops pulled his blackened glass pipe from his pants pocket. Putting his stone on top of the brillow he lit it with a Bic lighter, making the crack sizzle as he inhaled the smoke into his lungs.

Floss looked at Pops, watching the effects the crack had. The man finished, smacked his lips, and blew out a thick cloud of smoke.

"Come on Pops!" He said waving his hands to fan the stench.

"My bad but ain't this my spot?" The crackheads eyes were bulging out of their sockets.

"Let me use the phone," T-Roy said heading to the kitchen.

"Go on," the old man said.

For an old man that smoked crack for as long as he had, Pops had a nice place and tried to keep it up as much as possible. One thing for sure that was fucked up was his old ass table that always seemed to have some type of crack residue on it.

Pops had been in the hood ever since Floss' mom and dad were kids. He was old like his grandparents.

"Man Pops, you be on that rock mornin', noon, and night. Don't you eat?" Floss asked him.

"Eat? Boy this here," he said holding up his pipe, "Got all the nutrients I need. See boy, look how big my muscles are, and how healthy Pops look."

Floss just shook his head looking at the unhealthy, frail man that sat in front of him. T-Roy was on the phone talking all fly. After getting talked out of another hit of crack from Pops, the two homeboys left to hang out to get some chicks.

Shirley was another known smoker from Freetown. When they offered her a rock to give them a ride, she was more than willing. T-Roy's chick was Keke, she stayed up the road off of Ritchie Highway and Jumpers Hole Road. Once they got to her house, they picked her and her girlfriend Tia up. Floss had seen Keke before, but never had he seen Tia. At 5'8, she was about his height, around 135 lbs., all ass and hips, with light brown eyes, and a light complexion. She was mixed with Black and Cuban.

"Hey y'all," Keke said, smiling as they both crammed in the back seat. "This is my home girl Tia."

Right off the jump, Floss and Tia locked eyes. He could tell she was feeling him, even though he was a year younger. Shirley played chauffeur and drove them to a place called Honey-Bee's for some food. T-Roy was in full mack mode trying to convince the girls to go to the motel with them. Finally, he broke them down and in no time they were in two separate rooms chilling out.

Floss could tell Tia was shy. As she sat on the bed, looking pretty he said, "You don't gotta be all nervous. Relax."

She giggled, "I ain't nervous." But he could tell she was.

The phone rang and it was T-Roy., "What's up homie?"

"Man slide down to my room right quick."

"Alight." Floss figured something was wrong because he heard some aggression in T-Roy's voice. He hung up and turned to Tia, who was relaxing on the bed watching television. "I'll be right back."

He left his room and made it to T-Roy's. When his partner opened the door he could sense the tension between Keke and T-Roy.

"What's up y'all?" Floss asked.

T-Roy's face was twisted up as he nodded towards Keke, who looked sad as she laid on the bed.

"Your homeboy is tripping," she said.

T-Roy said, "Shorty ain't shit, son. Every time she comes around me it's about money. She swear she needs something, like I'm a trick nigga."

Keke smacked her lips. "I just asked for thirty dollars to get my nails done."

Floss stood there while they went back and forth. It was like a tennis match. "Look T-Roy ain't nothing wrong with helping her look well. That's your chick. She's down for you."

"Yea," came Keke., "How come you can look fly but I can't!" Her comment started up the arguing again.

"Aye yall," Floss said. "Chill out. I'm going back to the room with Tia. We got these rooms, so yall need to enjoy the time."

Floss walked out and headed back to his room. When he got there he heard the shower running. Feeling good about getting him some, he stripped down to his boxers and got in the bed. He was watching an old rerun of Martin when he heard the shower water cut off. A moment later, Tia exited the bathroom wearing nothing but a towel. He smiled. Something caused her to pause, as she stopped in her tracks.

"What's wrong?" he asked.

A nervous look spread across her face again. "Uh......."

He patted the bed. "Come over here."

Moving hesitantly, Tia made her way over to the other side of the bed. She stood there for a moment, just looking at him. Her eyes were on his naked chest.

"Why you looking all scared?"

Her eyes dropped then she said, "Cuz, I know we was supposed to come kick it. But I ain't know we was coming to a room, and I know what you expect."

Floss sensed she was really scared. "So what's up, you don't wanna chill?" His words held a double meaning.

She shrugged. "I mean... I don't want you to be mad. I really like you, so...."

He remained silent. Tia looked, and all of a sudden dropped the towel, exposing her naked body. Then moving fast she got under the covers.

He laughed. "Why you actin like you've never done this?"

She got mad. "Because... I haven't!"

Her words caught him off guard. "What?? You mean...?"

"I'm a virgin," she replied boldly. "But I'm old enough, and I know what I'm ready for. It's just..."

"What? It's just what?"

Tia took her time before she spoke. "It's just, I want you to take your time. Because I know it's gonna hurt."

Floss was in total shock. He knew by her facial expression she was telling the truth. She was scared. For a moment, they just stared into each other's eyes until finally they closed in for a passionate kiss. Something inside of him moved as he felt a fire burn deep between them.

Tia looked him in his eyes and said, "I'm ready."

Floss had never been with a virgin before and to him this was special. Wanting to take his time, he climbed on top of her and paid attention to all the signs her body gave him. Though he was young he did his best to keep control. He would never forget the experience of making love to Tia for this first time. That night, they spent hours afterwards talking about things he had never spoke about, to any other female. He was really feeling her.

Floss and Tia started spending a lot of time together. Being the player T-Roy was, he felt his young partner was getting pussy whipped.

"If I'm feeling her, then that's me," Floss explained as they walked through the mall.

It was T-Roy's birthday and he was feeling himself. "Man you be feeling all these money hungry chicks."

A few females passed them, smiling and flirting with their eyes. It was a Saturday and Marley Station Mall was packed. From all the hustling he had been doing, T-Roy looked to spend a few dollars on an outfit, to go to a club called Twilight Zone. It was a spot where they could definitely get in, despite all the events going down inside and their age.

They were walking out a Footlocker when they saw six guys mean mugging them. They recognized them to be from Pioneer City, and Meade Village. The two hoods ran together against those from Freetown.

"You see those niggas?"

Floss nodded. "Yea."

Making a right turn in the opposite direction, Floss looked back over his shoulder and before he knew it the small group surrounded them.

"Aye nigga!" "Do you remember me?" one called out talking to T-Roy. The cat's face was twisted all up. He was short with a nappy afro.

"I'm the nigga you and your punk ass homeboys jumped in the club!" Hearing this, Floss balled his fists, ready for a brawl. The other dudes surrounded them.

Quick on his feet, T-Roy replied. "Oh yeah? Well, we got niggas all around this bitch, if y'all wanna trip!" Then he placed his hands beneath his Baltimore Ravens jersey. "Plus, I got this hammer on me... Who want it?"

For a split-second, the group paused. Floss forgot about the gun, not knowing T-Roy was carrying it. One of the guys standing to T-Roy's left took the chance and swung, catching him on his blind slide and knocking him off balance.

"He ain't got no gun!" Somebody called out.

Floss swung and hit a guy before getting rushed by three. Just that fast a fight broke out right there in the middle of the mall. T-Roy tried to retaliate the best he could but continued to get assaulted by the flurry of fists until he fell. Floss looked up and saw him on the ground getting stomped, then one guy caught him square in the face sending him to the ground as well.

"Here comes the mall security!" Someone yelled.

Floss and T-Roy were badly beaten but still they managed to get to their feet.

"Come on, let's go." Floss said, helping his homeboy to his feet. Responding to the incident, mall security detained the two with cuffs and took them to a side room for questioning. Neither answered anything and after an hour they were let go. Both of them jumped in T-Roy's mother's car and he put the new Tupac CD in, before cutting up the volume.

"I won't deny it... I'mma straight rid'ah... You don't wanna fuck wit' me.. Got the po-po bustin' at me... But you can't do nothing to a Geeeee..."

When they pulled into their hood and parked, Floss looks at his partner and asked, "Man why you pump fake like you had the gun, where is it at?"

With a swollen eye, T-Roy said angrily, "I let Nell use it and he had to toss it when the police were chasing him."

"What?" Floss was pissed. "How you going to let another nigga use the gun we bought without asking me first?"

T-Roy wasn't trying to hear it. "Son, ever since you started fucking with that bitch Tia, you've been bugging."

"What my girl gotta do with this? Keep her out of it."

"So, she's your girl now?" T-Roy ask in a sarcastic tone.

The frustration they both felt for what happened at the mall became the real reason behind them arguing. For twenty minutes they sat in the car going at it until Floss had enough.

"Look, it's your birthday and we're up here arguing."

T-Roy was now looking in the rear-view mirror at his swollen face. "Man, I wanna go kill those niggas."

"How?" Said Floss. "We ain't got no gun!"

"I know, I need to get one."

"Shit, call that nigga Los. You said he got your back. Well, now is the time to find out."

T-Roy got extra excited. "Oh, if I call him, he'll get shit poppin'!"

"Well call him then."

On the spot they drove up to the Chinese Liquor Store. T-Roy used the payphone to call up Los, to tell him what happened. He explained everything in detail and told him they needed some guns and back up.

"Nigga, what the fuck I look like?" Los barked. "Where's that money for the work I fronted you?"

T-Roy was caught off guard. "... Man, I still got some coke left.... But..."

"Well call me back when you got my money then!" Los hung up in his face. Floss could tell by the expression T-Roy wore that things didn't go as planned.

"He ain't coming huh?"

T-Roy was really mad now. "Man fuck that nigga. All he cares about is the money I owe him."

"The money you owe him? For what?"

"For the work he fronted me."

Up to that point, Floss was under the impression his homeboy bought his own crack. "Man all that hustling you be doing and you still getting fronted?"

He nodded. "Yeah."

"I thought you was getting money like that." Floss was surprised at this information.

"I know." T-Roy replied, "But that's why I Los meant so much to me."

"Well, fuck that nigga! For real, T-Roy! Whatever it is you owe him, fuck that.... You keeping that shit. He's a bitch ass nigga anyway. You see he ain't got cha' back like that."

"But who else is gonna give us work?"

Floss shook his head. "It's a million niggas to cop from, yo! I saw a niggah punk that nigga Los. He's a pussy. Whatever it is you owe, keep it. If he comes trippin', we'll fuck him up!"

T-Roy had no words. "Now, fuck this... It's your birthday. Let's go have some fun."

And despite looking like they both fought Tyson, they set out to have a good time; partying off the money owed to Los.

CHAPTER FOUR

Back at the holding facility.... Present Day

F loss was sitting in the cell giving Miles a rundown of events from his early days in the game. His head was hurting trying to figure out who was snitching on him. Miles looked over the informant list Boodah shot over to check out, trying to see if he recognized any names as well.

"So this nigga T-Roy... You don't see his name on here?"

Floss shook his head. "Nah, that's my right hand man."

Miles gave a sarcastic grunt. "Shit, those are the main ones to watch."

"Yeah, I've been thinking about that."

"Y'all weren't even on like that back then." Miles observed.

"Nah, we weren't."

Placing the list on the desk, miles asked, "What's up with that nigga Los? You said he was a bitch for real. Maybe it was him."

Floss got up and leaned against the wall. "Man, that pussy ass nigga turned out to be some cold shit. After he showed his true colors to T-Roy, he turned around and pulled a gun on my boy."

"Oh yeah? For what?"

"That money T-Roy owed him. And, guess what?"

Miles was already waiting.

"He used the same gun we bought from that smoker." Floss shook his head.

"Apparently, T-Roy partner Nell, was there when Los confronted him. And since Nell also sold coke for Los, when he asked for the gun, Nell passed it to him."

Miles looked unfazed. "And, those niggas was supposed to be boys."

"All of us were." Floss told him. "Los was older and Nell was about T-Roy's age. That's why I say Los used his age to manipulate a lot of us young niggas. At the time, we admired the big homies who had fly shit. But I was wiser than that, and saw through that nigga."

"So what happened when he pulled a gun on T-Roy? Did he shoot?"

Floss looked up with a devilish grin as he spoke. "Nah... T-Roy shot off like a rocket, running into the woods. From that day forward it was fuck Los! Then a turn of events transpired that led to his downfall, and our rise in the game."

Miles was intrigued. "Oh yeah?"

He nodded. "And I became the man, building my first crew at the age of sixteen. Whoever it is telling on me, they could go back that far. Who knows?" But Floss knew if they did go back that far it could mean more charges against him.

1997

Introduction into the Game

CHAPTER FIVE

Floss had other family members who lived in Freetown. His grandma had a house on New Freetown Road and his five uncles', Marty, Junebug, Meatball, Stump, and Pook hung out like everybody else. His uncle Pook was a crackhead who grew up with all the OG's and was well respected in the streets from all the work he put in, and he found ways to squeeze money and drugs out of niggas on the block. He was known to rob niggas with only his dog if he thought you were a pussy. He was the Debo of the neighborhood and niggas knew better than to try and cross him. So, when T-Roy couldn't find anybody to hook them up with some more coke they called on Pook. He helped them out a few times, but it was months later that Floss' other uncles really hooked them up.

Freetown was alive with crackheads driving in and out the hood coppin' work. Floss and T-Roy was chilling at his grandma's house in the front yard. Her two-story yellow house was known by everyone, as well as her. She was known to keep big guns and had a reputation to shoot at whoever tried her patience. It was the top of the year and cold out so the two homeboys huddled out front, contemplating who they were going to get some coke from.

"Hey yo, whose whip is that?"

Floss looked in the direction T-Roy referred to, and saw a 97' all black GS Lexus 400 on 20 inch rims coming up the street. Then to their surprise, it pulled into his grandma's driveway. His uncle Stump and the driver hopped out the passenger's side, making their way towards the house.

"What's up y'all?" Stump called out.

They nodded.

"Who's that?" T-Roy asked.

Floss looked at the driver of the Lexus. He was a large man, tall and stocky. He'd seen him before in another car, also recognizing his face, from another place and time.

"I think he's an old friend of my pops."

"Shit...he looks like he's on! Did you see that fat ass platinum chain and cross? That bitch got diamonds blingin' all in it!" T-Roy said in admiration.

Both of them knew Stump was hooked up with a few ballers. So Floss suggested they follow them inside to see if they could learn more about the dude.

"Heeey, Big Don. How've you been?" Came the voice of Floss' grandmother. As soon as he entered the house, Floss saw the guy his uncle was with hugging his grandmother.

"I've been well Ms. Shirley, and you?" He said

She shrugged. "Fairly well." She looked at her son, as Stump headed to the kitchen. "Keep yo ass out my greens!"

"Alright Ma." Stump replied.

Floss and T-Roy walked past them and went to the living room. They saw this guy called Big Don go into the kitchen with Stump and his grandma, as the three of them took seats at the table. Floss overheard the guy mention his father, and he peaked around the corner in time to see Big Don hand his grandma a fat wad of money.

T-Roy nudged him. "I'm telling you, he's on big time." He went on to tell Floss how Los told him about a cat who drove an all-black GS Lexus, that he bought this work from.

"You think it's him?"

"Maybe so. Let's find out." T-Roy said as he shrugged.

After putting a battery pack in Floss' back, the two of them waited for his uncle Stump and Big Don to finish with his grandma. They could be wrong, but because it wasn't anyone to buy coke from, they figured it couldn't hurt to find out for sure if Big Don could be a possible plug.

Big Don and Stump were hanging out in the driveway, next to the Lexus when they came out of the house.

"Wussup, nephew?" Stump called out.

Floss looked at his uncle. "You know, just holdin' it down out here."

Stump nodded at T-Roy and said, "You better be takin care of my nephew lil nigga."

He laughed. "Shit, big homie, he lookin out for me. Everybody knows Floss is ahead of his time." T-Roy stepped towards the Lexus and looked at Big Don who had been silent up to that point. "Man this bitch is clean. What year is it?"

"It's a nine-seven," Big Don replied with a boss like swagger. "Why, you tryna' cop it?"

That's when Floss stepped forward. With confidence he said, "Hell yeah! As soon as we get this money off these streets, we just might holla at chu."

Big Don looked at his little ass and then to Stump. "Man, your nephew is a mutha fucka."

Stump laughed. "And, he's as serious as a heart attack."

"You're Big Mike's son, huh?" Big Don asked.

Floss nodded. "Yea, and yea I'm serious. Me and my boy T-Roy, once we get back on with a consistent plug, we'll cop that nine-seven. No prob."

"Yea," came T-Roy.

Big Don took a good look at T-Roy and said, "Don't you fuck wit that nigga Los?"

On cue, T-Roy's mood changed. "Fuck that nigga! I use to but his bitch ass pulled a gun on me, and I was his most loyal runner."

Floss added, "Since then we ain't fucked with him. That's why we're lookin' for another plug."

Big Don looked at him and asked, "Lil nigga how old are you?"

"Sixteen."

"Does Big Mike know you out here hustlin'?"

He nodded. "My pops knows I'm cut from the same cloth as him."

"What about Bell? Does she know?"

At the mentioning of his mother's name, Floss knew the man was well aware of who he was. "She knows I'm the man of our house. That's what she knows."

Big Don looked at the two youngsters and seemed to contemplate a few things.

"Let me ask you somethin', Big homie," came T-Roy "Why you ask if I knew Los? I know he used to mess wit chu. Is that your boy?"

Now it was Big Don's turn to diss the man. "That nigga owes me and when I catch him I'mma do something bad to him."

"You used to hit him off, huh?" T-Roy asked next.

"Hit him off? I'm the reason why he's broke right now and in hiding. He owes me big time."

Not holding his tongue Floss said, "Well, we know how to bring him out of whatever cave he's been duckin' in. How about we make a deal?"

"What kind of deal?" The man asked intrigued at the offer.

"If we can bring him to you, how about you work with us," Floss suggested. "It don't take no rocket scientist to see you're the Head Nigga In Charge around here."

The comment flattered Big Don who looked at Stump. "I like these little niggas," he said laughing. Then he got serious. "You know what, I'll make y'all a deal. If you can bring Los to me, I'll see what I can do. But I'm not gonna lie," he looked at Floss. "Big Mike is my man from way back. If for any reason he says not to fuck wit you, then I'mma honor that."

Floss nodded. He was confident that he and T-Roy could bring Los out of hiding. He also felt his pops wouldn't have an issue with him dealing with the OG, as long as he kept it 100%. His father

always stressed to him; if he was going to be in the streets, he had to honor it as a grown man's game. "Okay, I'm wit it."

Later that night, he and T-Roy plotted on how they were going to make this possible. He had a good idea and when he shared it with his partner, T-Roy wasn't so sure it would work.

"Man what if something goes wrong?"

Floss wasn't second guessing it. "Trust me, it'll work."

"Do you think Big Don will really hit us off?"

He knew all of T-Roy's doubts were because he was nervous. Despite being younger Floss remained confident. "He will. My pops never fucked with fake nigga's. You see how he stopped by and looked out for my grandmother? Big Don is a real nigga. We need to focus on getting Los. The rest will come together. Now, come on. We got some fishing to do."

"Fishin'?"

Floss nodded. "Yea... We're about to catch us a bitch ass nigga."

CHAPTER SIX

Floss and T-Roy were posted up on Levy Court. It was just after 6 o'clock in the evening and everybody was out. Hustlers and hood rat chicks hung out as crackheads pulled into the courtyard looking to score. The two homeboys were chilling, looking up and down the street patiently.

"Are you sure he's coming?"

T-Roy looked at Floss and said, "He told me he was. As soon as I told him I had his money he stopped cussin' and shit, askin' me where I was. I told him in the hood, up in Levy Court. Man, he sounded like he didn't wanna come down here though."

Floss laughed. "Big Don was right. He tryna' lay low."

The two stayed outside the apartment building for another thirty minutes before they saw a green J-30 Infinity pull into a parking space in front of the building.

"I think that's him," said T-Roy.

Floss saw Los in the driver's seat. "Yep! Aye, stall that nigga while I call Big Don."

While T-Roy did as he asked, Floss shot into the building and headed to a crackheads house named Ms. Shirley. Giving her a dime rock, she let him use the phone to call Big Don.

"You got him there now?" The OG asked.

"Yea, T-Roy is out in the courtyard with him now. He's driving a green J-30."

"Okay, I'll be there in a hot minute. Just keep him there."

When Floss hung up the phone, he turned and saw Ms. Shirley sucking on the end of her glass pipe. Fire blazed from her lighter as she hit the remainder of the rock he gave her.

Exhaling smoke with big eyes she said, "Oh you already done? Give me another hit and you can use the phone all day."

"Nah, I'm good." Floss shook his head and shot out of the house.

When he reached the building, Los was all up in T-Roy's face. He had a gun in his hand, at his side, checking the shit out of T-Roy. Floss saw how his homeboy had the look of fear on his face.

"Ayo Los!" he called out. "Come on man, we're homies!"

At the mentioning of his name, Los looked in Floss' direction. "Nah y'all little niggas think it's a game. Playin wit my money and shit."

T-Roy said, "Man I told you I got jumped on my birthday and had to go to the hospital." He lied.

Los twisted his face in anger. "Nigga yo ass is gonna be in the hospital alright."

Just when Floss though thought it was going to go all bad, two Hummer's pulled into the lot, screeching to a halt. Los, T-Roy, and Floss watched all eight doors fly open as Big Don stepped out with at least nine armed men; killers carrying AK-47's, Mac 11's, and handguns.

"Hold up nigga!" The OG called out as he aimed a desert eagle .45 at Los.

At the sight of Big Don, Los' demeanor switched up and he began to stutter. "Uh.. B-B-Big Don, uh I'm tryna' collect this money and bring it to you."

Big Don looked at T-Roy and Floss. "From these little niggas? They owe you ninety-seven large?"

Los opened his mouth to speak but before he could Big Don cut him off. "Take that pistol from that nigga and get him in the car."

Floss and T-Roy watched as Los surrendered the .9 mm to a man that was 6'4" and built like a WWE Wrestler. Then the others rushed him into a Hummer.

"Where you takin' him?" Floss asked Big Don.

The OG simply said, "Come and find out."

Big Don took Los to another building down the street, while everyone unloaded and went to one of the OG's trap spots. The inside of the apartment was empty, except for a few folded chairs and milk crates. To Floss, it looked like a place where they cooked or cut up work. The goons who had Los shoved him inside, making him fly into the drywall; which knocked a hole in the wall from the force. His body then crumbled to the floor.

"Pick his ass up and tie him up," Big Don ordered.

Doing exactly what they were told to do, the goons tied Los up with a thick wire. Despite his protesting, he was bound and gagged, then sat in one of the chairs.

"So," Big Don said standing before him. "You think I'm pussy."

"Mmmm.... Mmmm...Mmmmm," Los mumbled through the dirty rag that gagged him.

"Yeah, you do.".

Wham!

With a closed fist Big Don swung a mighty blow. All 285 pounds of him connected with Los, as he flew out of the chair.

"Mmmm!!!" he cried as blood spilled from his nose.

Floss heard bones crack. "Get his ass back up in the chair!!" The OG commanded.

Floss and T-Roy watched as Big Don beat Los like a punching bag. When his fists got tired, he had his man sock on Los; until his eyes and face were black, blue, and bloody. At any moment they expected Los to topple over and die.

The whole time they beat on Los, Floss was wondering what in the hell could he do to prove his loyalty to Big Don. In one thoughtless motion, he lunged for the desert eagle he saw Big Don place on the counter.

BOOOOMMM!!!

The lone slug barked loudly, startling everyone in the room. T-Roy jumped face first into the carpet with the gun recoiling from the kick it gave. Floss saw in slow motion as Los' entire face exploded like a watermelon, sending his body backwards in the chair. Blood and brains splattered the far white wall like a painter's canvas.

"What the fuck!!" Somebody yelled.

Big Don jumped out of the way as well. He turned and looked at Floss who held his gun in his hands. For a brief moment, everyone looked at him as if they couldn't believe what he just did.

CHAPTER SEVEN

Back at the holding facility...Present Day

L istening to Floss recount his story, Miles gave him a look of pure shock. "Damn nigga! You murked that bitch ass nigga, Los, in front of all them people?"

He nodded his head.

Miles stood up from the bunk and paced the cell. "You better thank God you ain't got murder charges."

"At least not yet," he said gratefully.

"That's the truth. Because these people will supersede a nigga with more charges in a heartbeat."

"Well, let's not talk that shit up." Floss exhaled a long sigh just at the thought.

"So," Miles began, "This nigga Big Don.. When you put that work in, did he look
out?"

"Hell yeah! I brought all this up to explain the day me and T-Roy really got on. Even though he didn't pull the trigger, I put us in a position for Big Don to become our main supplier."

Miles listened as Floss broke down how Big Don was thoroughly impressed with him. Combined with the fact that the OG knew both his mother and father, Big Don took him under his wing.

"First he started us off slow," he continued. "I guess after the incident with Los he wasn't going to put too much work in anyone else's hand, until they proved worthy. So he gave me sixty three grams of fish scale coke and showed me the game. How to whip coke into crack."

"That's it?? You just murked a nigga! At least he could've..."

Floss held up his hand. "I know, I know. But I was young and willing to prove myself. You know, a nigga was pullin' the trigger for fun. So, this was an initiation for me to prove myself, I wasn't trippin'."

Miles understood. "So back to ya boy T-Roy. What was he on?"

The thought made Floss smile. "Shit, he was happy as fuck. Once Big Don showed me how to cook it up, I came back with three thick blocks of straight dope. We went right to Pop's spot and chopped that shit up. You remember that song by Wu Tang?"

"Which one?"

"C.R.E.A.M."

Miles nodded as he rapped. *"Cash Rules Everything around Me, CREAM, get the money ... dolla-dolla-bills ya'll!"*

Floss laughed. "Exactly. That's the mindset we had. This was the birth of us as a crew. Murkin' Los and proving to Big Don how down I was helped me build my own crew."

Thinking back to that moment, Floss realized this was the point in his life where he invited people into his circle he really didn't know. Now years later, he was being snitched on; figuring out exactly who was telling was beginning to be more difficult by the moment. Trying to take his mind off of things, Floss started to get ready for his visit.

Not long after they started messing around, Tia and him got serious and they ended up having a son named Da-Da. With him being locked up, she held him down like a true soldier. Today she was coming to see him, and he wanted to tell her about the latest developments in his case.

"Yo, your shorty is running late ain't she?"

He nodded. "And she knows I don't play that." Already showered up, he waited to be called. Floss was on the phone trying to reach his lawyer. He'd been waiting an hour for Tia to make it up there, but she was still running late. The unit was alive with dudes playing cards and sitting around talking shit. Everybody was facing charges; acting as if they didn't have a care in the world. Unable to get his lawyer on the line, he hung up. That's when he heard his name called over the speaker.

"Inmate Blacksmith, cell number 222, you have a visit!" Miles looked over at him and gave him a head nod. "Have a good one."

Making his way to the door, he waited for a C.O. to come get him. When the officer arrived, he was taken to a small room and stripped of his clothes. Once he was inspected, he was then led to the visiting room.

Inmates sat at his sides talking to family members, friends, and loved ones through a thick Plexiglas window. Floss glanced over faces as he walked looking for Tia. Then he saw her and Da-Da sitting with smiles on their faces.

He took a seat. "Damn Tia, why you so late?" She looked beautiful with her press and curl. She was wearing a sexy tight little red dress with red heels to match. Tia was one of the most beautiful women he had ever laid eyes on and after having their child, her body seemed to enhance in all the right places. Tia was all hips, thighs, and ass with a sexy walk that made her ass cheeks bounce.

"No how you doin' or nothing, huh? Just why am I late?" she asked twisting up her lips.

He shook the stress he was feeling. "Sorry bae, I just got a lot of shit on my mind. But you look beautiful as always." He looked at his son. "What's up boy. Lookin' just like me."

At two years old, Da-Da squirmed in his mother's lap, smiling and reaching for the window.

"He misses you," Tia told him. "Last night he asked for his daddy."

The feeling he got hearing this only made his spirit sink. "I love you."

Da-Da said, "Love you too daddy."

"We would've been here earlier but he made a big mess on his clothes, spilling juice everywhere. His car seat got soaked," Tia explained.

He smiled at his boy. "That's right, give mommy a hard time like she does daddy."

She snapped. "Don't tell him that!"

Floss just laughed.

"Look, I spoke with your lawyer Mr. Ravernell and he's supposed to be up here today. He said he has some information about your case."

He nodded. "Yea, from what he told me there's a confidential informant on my case. I'm just waiting for him to tell me who it is."

"Who do you think it is?"

He shook his head. "For real, I don't know. But when I do...."

Tia knew him so she gave him a look and cut him off. There were too many people in there. "When you do, just sit back and relax. I'll be back to see you next week and we'll figure out what needs to be done."

That's why he loved her. She was his ride or die. Even though he had done her wrong by fucking on other chicks, she still had his back when he heeded needed her most.

For the next two hours, Floss enjoyed his visit until finally it was over. When he returned to the unit, he went to his cell to get some alone time, while his cellie watched TV. Tia telling him his lawyer was coming made him feel better. Hopefully he would get the information he needed so he could push play on getting rid of the snitch.

Floss didn't know when he fell asleep, but he did. Miles came into the cell making all kinds of noise.

"What time is it?" Floss asked.

"After three. Damn, I didn't know you were back from your visit."

Hearing the time, he got up and cursed. "Mutha fuckin lawyers bitch ass was supposed to come up here." He knew if Mr. Ravenelle hadn't made it by now, chances were he wasn't coming.

Miles agreed. "Nah, his ass might not come. What's your girl talkin' about?"

"I told her someone was snitchin' and she told me to be cool. But I need to find
out."

"I feel you." Taking a seat on the desk top Miles folded his arms. "Man, I couldn't stop thinking about that Los situation. You better be glad the feds ain't got you for that shit."

He nodded. "Fa sho."

"But since you brought it up, how do you think it could play a part in whose talkin'? I mean, if you don't believe it's T-Roy or Big Don, then who?"

Floss laughed. "Nah, it ain't them. I went back to that because, like I said, that's when I started really comin' up in the game."

With Miles paying close attention, Floss explained how all this could've possibly been playing a part. He didn't want to overlook someone, so he wanted to go through every aspect of his time hustling. Miles understood his point. He was looking at a lot of time himself and knew the importance of paying attention to detail.

"So Big Don blessed ya'll. What next?"

Floss said, "Shit, what you think came next? It was back to the block as usual."

"Nah," Miles said shaking his head. "You said ya'll built a crew. Maybe it was one of them."

After thinking for a moment, he remembered a certain individual and shook his head.

"What?" came his cellie?

"One of the niggas me and T-Roy put on brought all sorts of bullshit and beef to the hood. So, yea, now that you mention it, there's a possibility."

Just bringing the situation to mind opened up the discussion again. Floss' interest grew as Miles listened to the story, asking him questions that made him think back.

Could it be? He thought. Until Mr. Ravenell came to confirm the informant, the only thing Floss could do was retrace his steps, until he found a possible link.

CHAPTER EIGHT

24 hours after he killed Los.....

When Floss and T-Roy hit the neighborhood with the work Big Don gave them, they headed straight to Pops' spot. They found the old man inside with the other crackhead, a chick named Tina.

"What's the deal youngstas?"

Floss stepped inside with T-Roy behind him, both walking like they owned the city.

"We got some fire we need you to test out," Floss announced to the old head.

Hearing they had testers, Tina jumped off the sofa in the living room. The blonde wig she wore was tilted. At 40 years old she was frail, and looked as if she needed a good bath and meal.

"Ohhh, let me get a blast. I'll tell ya'll if it's any good," she said happily.

"Sit cho ass down!" Pops said closing the door. "Always wantin' something for free."

Tina sat, pouting her lips.

"Don't trip Pops," Floss said. We got enough for the both of y'all."

Floss went to the raggedy kitchen table and asked Pops for a plate and razor. When Pops saw the solid rock he pulled out, his eyes grew large. Floss dropped the rock on the plate, out of the plastic and it sounded off with a solid "clank". He hit a corner of it with the razor.

"Here you go Pops," he said giving the man a nice size stone. "Give Tina half of it."

Pops was about to protest but thought against it.

While the pipe heads went about their business, Floss and T-Roy sat at the table, cutting work and putting it in green baggies. All they heard was lighters flicking and the sizzle of crack.

"Tina don't start that shit!" Pops said.

Floss and T-Roy turned around to see what all the commotion was about. What they saw was Tina sitting there on the couch with her lips balled up tight, eyes bucked, staring at her skin.

"They on me," she said looking crazy. "They all over me!" Then she jumped up rubbing her skin and started running around taking her clothes off.

"Dammit Tina!!" Pops roared.

Floss and T-Roy watched as the woman went into a crack trip. She started yelling about how the bees were on her, trying to eat her alive. They just started laughing as she took off each article of clothing she had on, until she was butt ass naked.

Pops yelled at her. "Girl sit cho' ass down in my house! Runnin' around like you're a child! Put your clothes back on!!"

"They in my booty!" she cried scratching her butt.

Floss and T-Roy started laughing even harder. "Nigga we got that fire!" Floss told him. "We gon' make a killin'."

T-Roy nodded his head. "Yea, when they get a dose of this, the fiends are gonna go crazy as shit!"

Once they finished cutting up the work, they realized they needed more baggies. Tina damn near offered to sell them her car for another hit. Giving her a $10 piece, they jumped in her beat-up Oldsmobile Cutlass and headed to the store.

T-Roy was behind the wheel as they rolled through the hood. They saw two youngsters named Rock and DC posted on the block. Rock was from Freetown, Floss and T-Roy had known him forever, and they were all the same age. DC was from Annapolis and moved to Pasadena with his aunt who lived in Willing Court.

"What's up with yall niggas?" T-Roy said asked, stopping the car and hollering at the two.

Rock was short and stocky, a real goon type. DC was slim with short dreads and a long scar across his face.

"We just tryna' get this money," Rock said, approaching the driver's side window.

"What ya'll workin' wit?" Floss asked.

DC shrugged. "Just a few twenty rocks, after that we gon' re-up. We're tryna' get our paper up."

Seeing that he had Big Don on his line, Floss already had thoughts of selling the work he had to both smokers and small-time hustlers. He knew a lot of young hustlers within his hood who needed little double ups here and there. As long as he got rid of the shit he had first, he didn't mind making small profits in return.

"Where ya'll headed?" asked Rock.

"To Wawa's in Pioneer City," T-Roy said. "Yall wanna roll?"

Everyone knew of the beef between them and the niggas from Pioneer City but that didn't stop Rock and DC from going. This told Floss a lot about the two cats. T Roy had just mentioned them to him a few days prior. He said they were always on the block but needed someone to put them on.

Whipping through the traffic, they jumped on Highway Route 100. Once they got to Pioneer City they exited and were at the corner store in no time. Six dudes were in front of the store shooting dice. T-Roy parked and the four of them got out the car and went into the store.

"Will that be all?" the clerk asked Floss.

"Yeah," he said. They purchased baggies, two blunts for T-Roy, and each of them had a bottle of Mystic.

After the clerk rung up the total and Floss paid, they left the store, only to find a group of cats' hanging out in front of Tina's car. One was sitting on the hood, and another had a baseball bat.

"What the fuck is this?" DC asked T-Roy and Floss.

T-Roy said, "Man fuck these niggas. They don't want no problems with us."

"What the fuck is ya'll doing over here?" One of them asked.

As the four of them appreciated the car, the one sitting on the hood slid off. With a grimace on his face, he opened his mouth to say something slick. That's when Floss took the first swing, knowing what time it was.

Wham!!

The Mystic bottle broke, instantly knocking the guy to the ground with blood running down his face.

"Get them niggas!" one of them called out rushing at Floss, T-Roy, Rock, and DC.

T-Roy swung on the nearest to him while Rock and DC managed to subdue the guy with the bat. They somehow wrestled it from his grasp and were now beating him with his own weapon. The cat T-Roy hit, tried to swing back but Floss caught him with a right that stunned him. Despite being outnumbered four to six, the small crew got the upper hand on them.

"Hey! Hey! Get the fuck away from my store!" the clerk said running out and making a scene. "I already called the police!"

The six cats from Pioneer City were on the ground bleeding or already running off. Floss, Rock, and DC rushed behind T-Roy as he got behind the wheel of the car; the four of them laughing as they fled the scene. This incident brought a bond between them, and Floss told T-Roy he felt they should put Rock and DC down with them. He explained his vision of how they could help move the work Big Don put in their hands.

"The faster we sell this shit, the faster he'll see how valuable we are,." Floss explained. "Then he'll give us more. I'm tellin' you, with Los out of the way we'll run Freetown."

T-Roy smiled. "Damn little nigga, you're smart as shit. I say we get wit' them about it tomorrow."

This was the beginning of Floss' first crew. They called themselves The Four Horsemen.

CHAPTER NINE

B ig Don had a young crew that was all about that the money and Floss knew the OG saw it. The way he put the Four Horseman together was a stroke of genius, and him being young only impressed Big Don even more. He was born for this type of shit.

After he was given the 63 grams, Floss cut up all the crack and came up with forty-one hundred. Using Rock and DC, he gave them one hundred-dollar packs, letting them keep twenty dollars off of each. They were going through three hundred every day, making sixty dollars easily. T-Roy and Floss were more aggressive, trapping out of every smokers spot they knew. Sometimes sleeping there.

Every three days Floss began meeting with Big Don. He no longer needed help cooking the coke. Now he was teaching T-Roy. Together they would bust the work down, bag it up, and use Floss' grandmother house as a stash spot. She kept old rifles and revolvers in her basement and no one ever went down there messing with stuff. They borrowed two .38 specials so they always stayed strapped. A set of rules was outlined to Rock and DC, so they were all on the same page.

"Like Biggie had the ten crack commandments, we gotta get some shit straight," Floss told Rock and DC. All four of them were at T-Roy's grandmother's house.

"Yea," T-Roy said. "Yall see what it's hittin' for. We getting money. Niggas is hatin'. We need to know if ya'll really down with this shit."

"I'm down," Rock said quickly.

"Me too," DC followed.

Floss said, "Okay, well first thing is we gotta have each other's back, regardless of the situation. I know ya'll ain't got no gun right now, but we'll work on that. In the meantime, we got this for ya'll."

Going over to the counter, T-Roy grabbed the two cell phones and pagers, and passed them out.

"There ya'll go. Now we can stay in touch, no matter what." Floss saw the look of shock on their faces. "Everybody's number is already programmed in the phones."

"Damn, we're really legit now," Rock said checking out the new Sprint phone and Motorola pager he had.

"Big Don bought us these," T-Roy explained. "He said we got potential. All we gotta do is keep our circle tight, without any corners. That way we keep rollin' forward, leaving no errors for squares."

Their emergency code for the pagers was 444. Floss said if any of them had a problem, this was the code. After running everything down and handing out the devices, Floss and T-Roy issued them some work. Rock and DC were now getting 3.5 grams a piece to begin their day. The 8 ball usually held them for most of the afternoon and sometimes night. But they were slowly making a name for themselves as a crew, and before long the fiends would all be coming to them.

***

Floss was at home getting ready for a night out with Tia. Since the day they met and spent the night together, they had been spending a lot of time hanging out. He was getting out of the shower when he heard the phone ringing. His little sister, Kita, answered it.

"Momma!! Telephone!" she hollered out.

He was coming out of his room when he met his mother in the hallway. She gave him a serious look.

"Big Don is on the way over here," she said straight forward. "Is there anything you wanna tell me before he gets here?"

He had no idea where she was coming from, but deep down he had an idea. "Where you know Big Don from, Ma?" He asked. Floss wasn't a fool. He knew the OG knew her, if he was cool with his dad. But he asked anyway.

"Boy, I'm your mother. So I ask the questions around here!" Putting her hand on her hip, she gave him a serious look. "So let's try this again. Is there anything you wanna tell me before he gets here?"

Exhaling a deep breath Floss said, "I was gonna tell you when the time was right."

"Tell me what?"

"I've been hustlin'."

"Hustlin' how?" she asked curiously.

Not really knowing how to say it he just blurted it out. "I've been sellin' drugs. And I'm sorry I didn't tell you before. I know I can tell you anything. But I didn't want you to worry."

CHAPTER TEN

One day, Floss asked Big Don if he would hit him off with more than usual. It was a regular day, and the OG had five ounces that he was passing off to one of his movers that pushed weight for him. As Big Don was handing his mover the five ounces with one hand, he had his other hand out asking about the money off the last package he gave him.

"Yo, you know you owe me $3,750 for the last five," Big Don reminded him. "Yeah I know I owe you big homie," his worker replied.

"So, if you know you owe me, then where the fuck is my money?" He stated back with deep base in his voice.

"Well, what had happened was...."

Ssssmmmmmmaaaackkk!

The big hand that Big Don laid on his mover's face had an echo with it; enough to stop the few passersby dead in their tracks.

"Now get the fuck out of my face and come back when you got all $3,750 of my money, and not a dollar short!" The OG warned. Not missing a beat, he turned to Floss. "Hey, well, if it ain't your lucky day. I was gonna let that nigga get these five ounces, but he fucked up so it's yours now."

Surprised, Floss said, "Damn Big Don, now that's what the fuck I'm talking about."

Big Don smiled before asking, "Now why do you wanna sell weight?" Floss wanted to make sure he thought about what he was going to say, because he knew the OG was sharp.

"So, everyone could start coppin' from me."

They both walked towards Levy Court to chill in front of this young chick's spot, who also worked for Big Don.

The OG asked, "So you wanna be the man, huh?"

He nodded. "Just like you."

Big Don laughed. "Man, you're seventeen now. To get where I'm at, it will take you years in the game. But I like how you think. First, you need to tighten up that crew you got, because you're only as smart as your team."

Since putting Rock and DC on, Floss and T-Roy began to hear some disturbing things. Mostly coming from clientele; smokers who claimed the two were shorting them on the package. Even though he felt he was ready for whatever, he respected Big Don. So he took his words into consideration.

After Big Don left, Floss went to see what his crew was up to. He went down to Shirley Murphy Court but couldn't find Rock and DC. Then he searched the housing buildings looking for T-Roy but couldn't find him either. That's when his cell phone rang.

"Yo, Wussup?"

"Floss?" It was T-Roy's mom.

"Yes Ma'am. How are you?" "Not so good," she said. "They got T-Roy down at Annapolis jailhouse."

"For what!"

She explained how the police caught him in Freetown and locked him up for trespassing, because he was banned from the housing projects.

"That's crazy," he said. "I can't leave my boy in there like that. We gotta bail him out."

"Do you know a bail bondsman?"

"I'll find one and then call you back."

Floss called his cousin who gave him a bondsman named Diddy. They found out T-Roy's bond was $25,000, but they only needed $2,500.

"You'll be able to handle that Cuz?" she asked him.

"Yea, let me get with my other partners and we'll get the money up," he said.

Wasting no time, he set out to find Rock and DC. Earlier they weren't answering their phones or the 444 pages he sent them. Two hours passed and he still hadn't located them and he was beginning to get upset. He tried both of their phones over and over again. Finally, after a million times he got Rock.

"Hello?"

"Nigga where you at?" He was heated.

"We're at Lake Waterfront Park playing basketball. Why?"

Floss was well aware of the park. It was where they played basketball, football, and had all sorts of events. "Man, T-Roy locked up. I need to meet ya'll."

Lake Waterfront was just up the street, so it took them no time to get back to the hood. Floss was posted up by Pops' house when he saw them coming; both looked as if they had no care in the world.

"What's the purpose of having pagers and phones if nigga's ain't answering them?" he asked. "I'm tryna' get this bail money up for T-Roy."

"What they got him for?"

He took his time explaining what T-Roy mother told him. When he finished, he told them they only needed $2,500 to get him out.

"So," he said finally. "How much ya'll got on his bail?" Both of them looked at him like they had shitted on themselves.

"Shit, I ain't got nothing," DC said.

But Rock was a little more willing. "Got a few dollars saved. But that's it."

Hearing the two, Floss went off. "We're supposed to be a team! Family!" He looked at DC and saw he wasn't really concerned. "If ya'll ain't tryna' be down just say so."

"We down," came Rock.

"But" DC said, "Why would he put himself in that position, knowing what would happen if the police caught him over here. Even if I did have the money, he'd have to give me my shit back."

Floss didn't want to go back and forth but he made a mental note about DC. If he only wanted to benefit from their crew, but not be willing to help when hard times came, he had another thing coming.

Rock only had two hundred dollars and Floss put in the rest; everything he had. Him and his cousin went to see Diddy, who said he would get right on it.

"Give me by tonight... around eight o'clock. I'll have him out."

"Cool," Floss told the bondsman. Diddy was a young cat with his own business, something Floss admired. "Could you call me when it's done? I wanna be there with his mom when get gets out."

"Yea... I can do that."

After Floss gave Diddy his cell phone number, Floss got a call from Big Don as he was leaving. As soon as he heard the OG's voice, he knew something was up.

"What's this I'm hearing in the streets?" Big Don asked.

"I don't know. What did you hear?"

"Come on little homie... don't play me like a fool. Ya boy T-Roy got knocked out there hustling?"

"Oh nah, he wasn't supposed to be in those project's so....."

Big Don cut him off. "You know the streets tell me first-hand what happens, and I'm hearing he took them on a long ass chase. Are you tellin' me different?"

Floss didn't want him to think he was trying to cover up what T-Roy did, so he said, "I just paid Diddy to bail him out, Big homie. As soon as we pick him up, I'll see exactly what happened."

"Alright, make sure you do that. This game is cold and niggas getting knocked can turn into some foul shit, you feel me?"

He did. After reassuring Big Don he would fill him in, Floss ended the call. It amazed him how the OG seemed to know every move him and his crew made. Big Don had workers on the streets watching and reporting everything back to him. The hours that followed left Floss in a thoughtful state. After letting T-Roy's mother know the deal, he went to Pops spot, so he could make some money and get his mind right.

"What's up with youngsta?" Pops asked as he played the PlayStation they always kept there.

"My boy got locked up and my crew's actin' like they broke," he said. "It's just crazy how these niggas ain't loyal like that. Now I got Big Don questioning if I can trust them."

Usually Pops would want some crack but today he wasn't trippin'. "Listen, before Los' ass started hustlin', I schooled him and helped him come up. He served out of this same spot. Floss, these niggas nowadays ain't loyal to shit. Big Don's right. The only person you can trust is yourself."

Right then Floss really began to question the loyalty of both Rock and DC. As far as T-Roy, he felt in his heart he could trust him, especially with him knowing he killed Los. If T-Roy needed bond that meant he hadn't told on him to get out.

***

T-Roy's mom drove them down to Annapolis jailhouse when he was ready to be released. When Floss saw his partner, they both smiled as he got in the backseat.

"Yeah, you thought I was gonna leave you in there, huh?"

T-Roy shook his head. "Man, I thought I was hit!"

"Well," his mother began, "Floss is your real friend. He raised all the money and got a bondsman."

"Thanks!"

Floss waved him off. "Don't trip. Like I said we're family." He didn't want to bring up Rock and DC, so he waited until they were back at T-Roy's place.

They were chilling in the living room when he decided to bring up some issues. With his mother in the kitchen cooking, T-Roy explained how he ran when he saw the police coming after him. They were hot in the hood and knew his face from all those other times they'd pulled up on them hanging on the block.

"I tossed the few rocks I had left," he told Floss. "And I already put up the money I made, so they were extra mad I didn't have shit."

"Well that's good." Taking a deep breath, he said, "I went to ask Rock and DC about puttin' in to get you out, and them niggas ain't have shit. Rock had a couple dollars, but DC was actin' funny."

T-Roy said, "Aye, I ain't feelin' that nigga DC like that."

"Oh yea? Why?"

T-Roy took his time and explained the situation involving this chick named Amber. Amber was fucking with DC but was really cool with T-Roy. She said DC was talking reckless about them, saying he was the one making all the money and they were basically feeding him crumbs.

Floss jumped up. "Man fuck that nigga!"

"Hold up!" T-Roy said quickly. "That ain't all. She also said, she thinks he's planning on tryna' get us. When she checked him about going against us, because we're all homies, he slapped her. I was about to call you after I got off the phone with her, but that's when the police saw me. So I ran."

Floss' next question came after serious thought. "Do you think Rock is in on it?"

T-Roy shook his head. "I don't know. But I wanna find out."

This was the day they realized they would have to do something to DC before he tried something slick.

CHAPTER ELEVEN

"**H**ow much does that nigga owe us?"

T-Roy was driving Tina's car with Floss on the passenger's side. He looked over and said, "Four hundred."

Floss slid the .45 back and racked a round into the chamber. "If he ain't got that when we pull up on him, I'mma pop his ass." He was dying to use the new piece he had bought.

It was after 10 o'clock and despite only being out a few hours, T-Roy was ready to do what Floss wanted. They tried to reach DC on the cell phone and put 444 into the pager numerous times, but no answer. They reached Rock who claimed he hadn't seen him since earlier when they were all together playing ball. Floss told him to call if he saw him.

His phone rang. "Yo! Wussup?"

It was Rock. "Aye, come down to Shirley Murphy Court. Man, DC done did some bullshit."

Smashing down New Freetown Road, T-Roy and Floss pulled up in the courtyard. Cats were posted up, outside hustling, crackheads were pulling up left and right; some zombie out and begging for free hits. When they jumped out both T-Roy and Floss could feel something was up, so they had their pistols in hand. Rock was standing next to a beat up Honda Accord. One of their younger homeboys Rell, was next to him with a few others. The youngster was holding the side of his face, where blood was coming from. It was obvious something happened.

"Wussup?" Floss asked approaching the group.

Rock stepped to them. "I just came from down here, after I spoke to you and the lil homie Rell said DC just left."

"That nigga blindsided me across the face with a thirty-eight," Rell called out angry as hell.

"For what?" came T-Roy.

"Tryna' serve my people," the youngster explained.

Rell told them a smoker had paged him for a sale and asked him to meet. Rell told them to meet him in the courtyard. When they pulled up, he went towards the car to serve them, but DC came from out of nowhere bombarding and demanding they but his coke.

"When I said something to DC and went to give my peoples the three stones, I had for them, the nigga whacked me."

Floss pulled up on Rell and said, "Don't trip, we got that nigga. If anybody sees him, know this; he's not a part of our crew anymore. Pop that nigga on site sight or call me and I'll do it."

Once they got done speaking to Rell, the youngster went back into his project unit. Wanting answers, T-Roy and Floss turned their attention to Rock.

"Tell me," Floss began. "What's up wit cha' man? All this shit he's pulling... you mean to tell me you didn't know about it?"

Rock shook his head. In defense he said, "Yo, that nigga is runnin' around here on some renegade shit, Floss."

"Did you know about him slappin' the homegirl, Amber?" T-Roy asked.

He nodded. "Yeah, but I didn't want to get in their business."

T-Roy whipped out the .38 special and aimed it right at him. "You be wit that nigga every day. How you ain't know he was talkin' shit? As far as we know, you was talking shit wit' that nigga!"

T-Roy was mad as hell. The pistol in his hand was steady, pointed directly at Rock's forehead. Floss just stood there looking to see if he read any signs of Rock lying.

When he felt he wasn't Floss asked, "So you're loyal to who?"

"Ya'll! The Horseman!"

Floss looked at T-Roy and told him to lower the gun. "Okay, well then, we want you to post up out here. If you hear anything or see that nigga, hit us immediately."

Rock promised he would and then they left.

Floss got a call from Tia saying she was over Amber's house, because she was scared to be alone. Him and T-Roy were on their way over there anyway, hoping to get some information as to where else DC might be. When they got there the two girls were chilling in the living room.

"His people from Annapolis are out here," Amber revealed. "I think that's what got him so cocky."

Floss knew DC relocated to Pasadena because he was getting into too much trouble in Annapolis. He was originally living with his aunt in the townhouses in Freetown, but she moved back to Annapolis. He stayed because of his relationship with Amber. Now she was saying they broke up and she had no idea where he was.

"Who are his people?" T-Roy asked.

"A few of his cousins. One of them just got out of the feds, and he's supposed to be out here to sell drugs," Amber explained.

Tia was sitting on the couch next to her. She looked at Floss and said, "That nigga is foul. Whatever ya'll do, be careful."

He knew Tia was concerned about him, so Floss did his best to assure her that they knew what they were doing. "Just stay with her."

Amber's face was swollen on one side. Tia thought it would be a good idea if she came to stay with her at her mother's house, and Floss agreed.

"If that nigga tries to contact you, call me. Okay?" he told her.

Amber said she would and then they left.

***

Days passed and no one had heard from or seen DC. Floss didn't care anymore about the money he owed him. He really wanted to kill him. But business had to continue, so he bust down the five ounces into grams and rocks. Although he was still upset with Rock, he kept him on the team. It didn't take long for Floss to see Rock really wanted to prove himself. He was moving $100 packs left and right.

T-Roy called him one night because it was rolling in Levy Court. Since they were young and gettin' it in the hood, that brought more of the hustlers out. Their homeboys Jay Rock, Wayne World, Rusty, Rico-Suave, Buddy B, and Rocky started posting up too. Each man was from Freetown as well but moved in their own packs and groups. Floss liked to stunt on them since he was one of the youngest. So, when he got the call, he shot down there ASAP.

Using a cluck head's brand-new BMW for the day, Floss pulled up and jumped out. Rico-Suave and Jay Rock were out front.

"Damn, lil nigga! Like that!"

Laughing Floss said, "Nah, it's a pipe heads rental. Where's T-Roy?"

Right then, his partner stepped out of the building. "Yo, you got some work?" Rusty and four more of his homies were there.

"Hell yeah. What's up?"

T-Roy smiled. "Man, its rollin'!"

Hearing this, Floss went to work. Despite him not seeing any fiends when he pulled up, it was like the crack in his pockets pulled smokers in like honey to bees. For two hours straight, sales came from both ends and before he knew it Rock was running down the street every five minutes for another hundred pack. Floss and T-Roy ended up busting down the grams and got an extra $50 out of each. It was rolling indeed.

Floss was sitting in the beamer counting money. T-Roy came over and opened the door.

"How much is that?"

Flipping through the wad, Floss said, "Almost nine racks. I gotta call Big Don for some more and to slide him this bread."

"Are we out?"

He nodded. "Yea. Let me call the big homie."

When he hit Big Don the OG gave him some bad news. He was out of work also. Floss knew that meant a lot of spots would be in trouble. From Pasadena, Glen Burnie, Annapolis, all the way to Baltimore, and that meant it would be a drought.

"What we gon' do?" asked T-Roy.

"Shit, we just gotta chill."

Well chilling turned into weeks. With the summer rolling around, Big Don apologized but he figured his people would've came through by then. In the meantime, he was riding down to Myrtle Beach for Bike Week. He promised by the time he came back they'd be straight. So Floss was instructed to relax.

They were in front of Big Don's sister's house, loading bikes on a trailer, when a red Camaro rolled by that no one had ever seen before. It really grabbed Floss' attention when the driver made a U-turn. Three black dudes in their early 20's twenties were in it.

"Who are those niggas?" Jay Rock asked T-Roy.

Rock said to Floss, "Remember I was tellin' you about them niggas I saw down in Willing Court? That's them."

Days before, he told Floss some mysterious dudes were down the street at this smokers' house serving coke.

T-Roy said, "That bitch Pleasure said they're from Annapolis."

"They got coke?" Floss asked. "Who they getting coke from? Who's their people?"

Jay Rock said, "That nigga y'all been lookin' for. What's his name?"

Floss looked at T-Roy. "DC?"

"Yeah, that's him."

Buddy B walked up, "Ayo, who's them niggas in the red 'Maro?"

Floss had heard enough. There was no way he was going to let these niggas come on his block and get money, especially when he wasn't getting a piece of it. "Come on, let's shoot down there and get these niggas straight."

Buddy B had a money green Suburban on 22's with limo tint. So when all five of them piled in, they rolled down the street, beating bass like normal. When they got to Willing Court Floss saw the Camaro and two cats standing in front of a townhouse.

T-Roy said, "Man... that's..." Before he could finish his sentence, Floss was hopping out the side door.

BOOM!! BOOM!!

When DC saw the .45 in his hand, he ducked behind the Camaro just before the first shot rang out. The other cat with him ducked but came up returning fire.

POP...POP...POP...POP

Buddy-B swerved the Suburban and everybody hopped out firing shots at the house and the niggas ducking. DC came up firing wild rounds hitting the side window of the truck, causing it to shatter. Floss ran up and let off two shots that hit the other guy.

BOOM!! BOOM!!

One bullet hit him in the chest and the other chipped the brick wall of the house. The dude flew backwards behind the car. Floss saw DC dash behind the townhouse.

"Get that nigga!" Jay Rock yelled.

A few of them ran after DC but he was too fast and they lost him. Someone called the police but before they could arrive, they all piled back in the Suburban and sped off. Buddy-B parked, and they hid in a female's apartment on Levy court.

CHAPTER TWELVE

Back at the Federal Holding Facility.... Present Day

Floss was at the slider talking to Boodah. The two of them were communicating every day, to update one another the latest developments in their case.

"All I've been doin' is thinkin' about this shit," he told Boodah. "My cellie and I been up all night. My lawyer still hasn't sent me the name of the nigga testifying against me. His bitch ass is supposed to be comin' up here!"

"I don't even recognize some of these niggas on my shit," Boodah said. "I mean, you don't have any idea?"

"Nah, I mean... I was thinking of one nigga. This cat named DC. Last night I told my cellie about him and he said it was possible. But it's been a minute since I see him." Floss laughed. "It's like he went into hiding. Plus these damn charges makes it seem like it's somebody else."

"Don't rule that nigga out. Trust me, when these niggas get caught up, they'll tell on anything and anyone. Even if it was some old shit," Boodah assured him.

A loud voice came booming over the intercom in the unit. "Get away from the slider!"

Floss stepped away quickly. He didn't feel like getting locked down for the day, plus he wanted to call Tia and check on their son. Miles was sitting at a table watching the news, and Floss took a seat next to him.

His cellie looked at him and said, "Man, I can't stop thinking about DC. How did that nigga just disappear? That was the last incident y'all had?"

"Nah his homeboys from Annapolis kept trying to come in our hood to get money," he said. "Our shit was pumpin' so they thought they could just get money without us buckin' like shit was sweet."

Floss went on to explain a situation that occurred when a chick named Shannon, who was from Annapolis, moved to Freetown.

"Once she got comfortable, her homeboys thought it gave them the right to come post up in Freetown. We had to go over to her spot and check them niggas. A fight broke out and Jay Rock slapped one of them with that iron, chipping the dude's tooth. Rico-Suave knocked another dude out cold, in front of Shannon's door."

"What about DC?" Miles asked.

He shook his head. "He never resurfaced."

Thinking to himself, Miles said, "Somebody probably knocked him off."

"Nah, I would've found out."

"Well, then you never know. It could be him."

Floss knew Miles was only trying to help, but not knowing who was snitching only kept him curious. The two of them sat there tripping off all the chaos going on in the city. Multiple homicides and robberies had occurred over the weekend, causing a few cats they knew to be arrested, dead, or just another unsolved case. The unit they were in didn't have too many blacks in it; most were whites and a few

Mexican and Puerto Ricans. Floss was thankful for the quiet unit, because he heard the bullshit on the other units daily. Just as he was about to get up and prepare for his daily workout, the officer working the control booth called his name over the loudspeaker?

"Blacksmith! Lawyer visit!"

Miles looked up at him and smiled.

The small room used for lawyer visits was a welcoming site sight to Floss. After the CO who led him there left, he took a seat. Mr. Ravenell, was already present. A little over 40 years old, the black man known to be one of the best trial lawyers in the State of Maryland; sat before him with an open folder, smiling like he had good news.

"Damn!" Floss said taking a seat. "My girl said you was comin' days ago."

"I know, and I apologize," he replied. "I was in trial and it lasted a little longer than expected."

Floss wanted to cut the chase and get straight to the point. "So, how's it lookin'? I was waiting for the information you said you were sending me. What happened?"

Mr. Ravenell gave him a patient look and exhaled a long sigh. "Okay, here's the deal, The US Attorney acquired an informant by the name of Andrew Stewart."

The name didn't ring a bell. "Man, I don't know anyone by that name."

"Well he knows you, and he's got information related to your drug charges. He's saying you two have done business," the lawyer said. "But that's the least of your problems. The government is now claiming to have another informant willing to testify, and possible conspiracy to commit murder charges on the way. Which also means you could now receive a mandatory life sentence if you blow trial."

The shock he felt was enormous. "Murder?" Floss dropped his head. "So now I got two informants to worry about?"

Mr. Ravenell nodded. "Yea and the government sounds confident they'll get a conviction at trial. Is there anything you want to tell me so I can be prepared?"

"Tell you like what? Man, I ain't kill no one," he said. "Or conspire to kill anyone. Who is this other informant?"

The lawyer shook his head. "I haven't been given that information. Mr. Stewart's name was difficult to obtain. But I'll tell you this, as long as these witnesses are willing to testify that hurts your chances of getting a reasonable deal. Right now, we need to think of a defense. Also, you need to inform me of any cars or houses you may have so I can help you protect them."

Floss exhaled a long breath and told Mr. Ravenell of the few things he had, that he didn't want to lose. His Benz, Lexus, Cadillac Escalade, amongst other cars, and the house he put Tia and his son in.

"That's in my girl's name though."

"The cars are in yours?"

"Yeah."

The lawyer wrote all that down. "I'll be back to see you in a few days. Until then, I suggest you begin writing down anything you feel may help your case."

Floss looked at him and said, "And that shit about coppin' to a deal... I ain't goin to prison because I ain't do shit, and I didn't get caught with shit! So you can tell the government to kiss my ass."

Mr. Ravenell wanted to object but Floss cut him off.

"I paid you a lot of money to do a job. So do it," he said firmly. "Get me that name and let me handle it from there."

When the session was over, Floss was escorted back to his unit. It was a little after two in the afternoon and everyone was either watching the news or playing cards like usual. He saw his cellie standing in the doorway of their cell.

"What's up?"

Miles looked at him and said, "Nothin'. Got a new nigga in the unit."

Floss looked over and observed a light skinned dude talking on the phone. He was a little taller than him, looked around 28, had a low cut, and a thick beard.

"Where's he from?"

"Annapolis. I hollered at him. The nigga is weird as fuck, on his sunni-shit."

Floss waved him off. "Anyway, fuck that, I got bigger problems."

"What's your lawyer talkin' bout?"

"This mu'fucka says I got another bitch nigga tellin'!!!" Floss entered his cell and closed the door.

"What???"

He nodded. "But I got the name of the other nigga. His name is Andrew Stewart."

"Do you know him? Are you sure that's not DC?"

"Nah. But whoever it is, he obviously knows me." Floss told Miles everything Mr. Ravenell explained relating to the government's case against him.

"Like I told you before, you need to find the witness. If you don't, these feds are gonna wash ya ass up."

"I know."

Feeling a little frustrated himself, Miles said, "Man if I had the resources to knock down the witnesses on my case, I would. Don't be like me, facing thirty years on a plea deal."

Floss wanted to inform Tia of the latest, so he gave her a call. He really didn't want to tell her the name of the guy snitching on him over the phone so he told her to come visit as soon as she could. When he got off the phone the new guy was hanging up as well, so he approached him.

"What's up man? You from Annapolis?"

The guy looked a little apprehensive. "Ah...yeah."

"What's your name? I'm Floss; from Freetown."

With a compassionate look he said, "I'm Abdullah Rasool Muhammad. Nice to meet you."

Floss gave him a sideways look. "That's what they call you on the streets?"

The man nodded. "Yes."

He shrugged. "Alright. If you need anything, let me know."

When he got back to the cell, Miles was laying on the top bunk, relaxing. Floss could tell he was in deep thought.

"Did you talk to your girl?"

"Yea."

"What you plan on doin'?"

"Shit tell her to have my homeboys find this nigga Andrew Stewart. That's for starters."

Miles said, "That's what I would do too. Ole' bitch ass nigga.... Murk his ass. Then that'll be one down."

"And one to go," he finished.

"Exactly." Miles turned over on his side. "So, after the shit with DC, who else can you think of, that might be tellin' on you?"

He folded his arms across his chest and took a seat on the desk. "So much shit happened, leading up to this point that I don't know."

CHAPTER THIRTEEN

Amber called Tia one day and said she had heard from DC. She wanted Floss to know she thought DC was going to snitch on them. Weeks later the police snatched up Rock, who was in a crack spot in Shirley Murphy Court. After that, Big Don told them to toss their cell phones because they may be tapped.

At the time Tia was pregnant so taking the money he had saved up, they moved into their own spot. Having Rock in jail meant he had to figure out a way to bail his homeboy out but his funds were low. Just as he was about to call Diddy, and make a payment plan with the bondsman, his mother called.

"Boy what in the hell did you do?"

He was confused. "Nothin Ma', what are you talking about?"

"The police just left my house looking for you," she said. "They want you to turn yourself in."

"For what?"

"They told me it's for two shootings. They were looking for you and T-Roy. They're saying ya'll are armed and dangerous."

"Ma', don't believe nothin' they say."

But she went off. "Boy how did you get yourself into some shit like this!" She barked. "I thought you were smarter than that. You're not thinking about me, Tia orthe baby."

Her words hurt him to his core. "Don't worry, I'll fix it."

"Okay, so, where are you? Because I need to come get you so you can turn yourself in."

Floss looked into the phone's receiver, wondering who was on the other end, because it couldn't be his mother.

"Boy do you hear me?"

"Yes, I hear you," he replied. "Are you jokin'?"

"Hell naw, I ain't jokin'!" Her voice went deeper than her usual soft sound. "Runnin' will only make you look guilty. If you go down there and show your face it will look better on you. Trust me, I'm the gangsta. You just get started."

Floss spoke to his mother more on the situation and when he was done he told her he needed to think on it. When he told Tia she just broke down crying until her eyes turned red.

"Didn't I tell you to quit sellin' that shit and get a job?" she asked, her voice trembling. "Look at me? Look at how big I am?"

"Baby calm down," he told her gently.

"I don't want to be like my friends, whose baby daddies are locked up!" She fell to the floor crying harder. "Why you do this to me?"

Floss' heart was broken. He didn't know what to do. He promised her he would figure something out. But turning himself in was out of the question. He couldn't risk Tia having the baby while he was in jail.

Feeling DC was behind all this, Floss left and called T-Roy from Pops' spot. When T Roy came and picked him up, his homeboy was already aware of the police looking for them.

"Damn, we didn't get a chance to get Rock out," T-Roy said.

"Yea, I know."

"Well look, I'm going up to Baltimore for a while and lay low."

"Where you gonna stay?"

"At this shorty's spot."

"For how long?"

"Until all this goes away."

Floss had a feeling it wasn't going to be that easy. "Well alright. Just send word to my people and let them know you're alright."

T-Roy looked at him and gave him some dap. "Yo, I got much love for you fam. Good look on your son comin'. Four Horsemen for life."

"For life."

The two were like brothers and Floss knew they'd catch back up. In the meantime, he decided to go back home and tell Tia his plan to leave town as well.

Floss had family in Eastern Shore, Maryland. After telling Tia they were going out there for a while he called his mom and then Big Don. The OG told him he'd support whatever decision he made, and when he returned, he'd still be there for him. His mother got the rental car for them and that same night they were on the road. Once they arrived at his Uncle Mack and Aunt Roxanne's house, Floss and Tia settled in nicely. Within three days, he had a job and was getting paid under the table, good money. But being on the run had them homesick. Tia's mother was pressing her to come back home and she was getting big really fast. Her mom didn't want her that far and having the baby. But the final decision was made when Floss called home.

"Baby T-Roy is locked up and their still comin' by here looking for you. They even asking our family members," his mother told him.

"Our family members?"

"Yea," she confirmed, "They've been over there at my mom's house harassing your uncles about you."

To hear the police were going by his grandmother's house was enough. "Alright ma', I'm coming home."

After two months on the run, Floss and Tia shot back to Pasadena. And despite his original intentions he turned himself in. The police reacted like they had finally caught the worst criminal America had ever seen. The shit even made the evening

news.

***

$180,000.

When the commissioner set his bond, Floss' head fell. He had been in Jennifer Road Detention Center for days and the zoo was becoming unbearable. But his prayers were answered when he got back.

After calling Diddy, Big Don paid the 10% and Floss' name was called to be released. Now a free man, he looked to repay the big homie and get his money back

Up.

"Violation?" He asked T-Roy's mom. He stopped by there to check on his homeboy. T-Roy had gotten released on house arrest but couldn't abide by his grandmother's rules, so his probation officer violated him.

Sadly, his mother said, "Yea, both me and your mother tried to talk some sense into him. But he's gotten too disrespectful. I just pray he learns his lesson while he's in there."

"He will," he assured her. "In the meantime, if you need anything, I'll be here for you."

Smiling she said, "Just stay out of trouble. Okay?"

"I will."

He had no crew. T-Roy was locked up. Rock had gotten five years for drug and weapon charges and he didn't know what else to do but hit the block solo-dolo. Even though he had a hood full of homeboys, Floss liked having his own team. But the show had to go on.

When he left for Eastern Shore, his mother relocated to another house. She didn't like the police always coming by. So, when he hit Big Don, he had the OG meet him over to the old house. To his surprise, someone had already moved in, so he waited a few houses down.

The cherry red Toyota Super on 20-inch chrome wheels rolled down the street beating hard as hell. Floss saw Big Don and stepped out to the curb.

"What's up lil nigga?"

Floss was smiling ear to ear. "Nothin' much, 96 limited editions," he said opening the passenger side door and getting in. The interior of the super felt and smelt good. Setting in he relaxed as Big Don pulled off.

"So, I see you out."

"Yea.. thanks man, forreal."

"It's nothing. Like I said before, I promised your dad and mom I'd look out." Taking a few side streets, Big Don rolled around so he could spend some time with him. "So, what now that your boys are locked up?"

Floss exhaled and said, "I don't know. But shit don't stop cause of this little situation."

"Oh, so this situation is little, huh?"

"Nah, my bad. It's not little. But I'm not gonna let it stop my flow." He looked at Big Don with a straight face and said, "I got a one-track mind, and that's getting this paper. My niggas need me right now, so I need you."

"Okay, so what can I do?"

"Man, Big Don, imma need a lot of work. I got to pay for our lawyers and some more shit. I got a baby due in about six weeks and I have to move my girl into another spot."

Big Don was impressed. "I see you're really serious and you know what? I got you. You know, I never got to straighten you out before I went to Myrtle Beach, with all that shootin' and shit. And yeah you need a lawyer."

"Do you have one?"

"Yea, I got you."

"What about the work? What can you hit me with?"

The OG just smiled. "Just relax. I got you."

Floss rode with Bog Don through the city until they entered a small residential area called Towson. There were nice homes with immaculate lawns with a quiet community and he knew you had to have money to live over here. Pulling in the driveway of a nice sized brick home, Big Don parked and ran in, only to exit minutes later with a Louie Vuitton backpack.

"Never bring anybody by here," he told Floss. "This is where I lay my head. I got baby mamas that don't know about this spot. Understand?"

He nodded. "Yea, I got cha Big Homie."

Big Don gave him a new cell phone and a business card that read: John Robinson, Esq. Attorney at Law. "Here call him tomorrow and tell him you're my people. I already got him retained in case something happens."

Floss placed both in his pocket.

Tossing the backpack on the floorboard at Floss' feet, Big Don asked, "Where can we cook this brick?"

A kilo? Damn! Floss' mind raced. Then he said, "Uhh shoot over to Marley Run. I got this shorty over there named Tiffany. She be low-key, we can use her stove." Moving through traffic, Floss couldn't help but to keep his eyes on traffic. He used the new phone to call Tiffany to ask her if she was busy. Knowing she stayed at home 247 or boosting clothes out of one of her friend's house, but she just happened to be home. He told her he was coming by with company.

"I'll be here," she said. "Why, what's up?"

He wasn't saying shit over the phone.

"I'll tell you when I get there." It didn't take long for them to pull up in Marley Run. Like always cats were chilling outside, shooting dice, and hustling. When they saw him and Big Don everyone looked in their direction and just nodded their heads as they headed towards Tiffany's apartment.

When Tiffany answered the door she saw Big Don and straightened up the stank look on her face. "Why didn't you say the big homie was with you?" she asked.

"Nah, not over the phone baby girl," Floss told her. "Is anybody here?"

She shook her head. "Only my son and he's asleep."

Tiffany was 20 years old, dark skinned and around 5'6. She was thick with a fat ass.

Tia couldn't stand her because she always hit on Floss. On late nights he'd post up at her spot from time to time to serve and smoke weed with her. He fucked twice, but it had been awhile since he had some of her wet pussy.

Stepping inside, Big Don closed the door. Floss said, "Let us use your kitchen to whip this work up."

"Yea," came Big Don. "I got chu babygirl."

Tiffany's parents grew up with Big Don so she knew him well. "Okay, go ahead."

Big Don looked at Floss. "Look I just need you to post up in the living room and watch the door. It'll take me no more than an hour to finish."

He hoped he could watch but he knew how to play his position. "Alright."

This was the beginning of a new era for Floss with no crew and a lot of responsibility before him he set out to hold it all down by himself. When Big Don was finished, he gave him 13 ounces to work with. From there it was all on him.

CHAPTER FOURTEEN

F loss was on a vicious grind. Using Tiffany's spot to hustle he managed to put Tia into another apartment in less than a week. Tiffany worked at Walmart, so she allowed him to use her Nissan Maxima to move about the city. She became his partner in crime, as well as a plaything. Although he loved Tia, Tiffany was his gangsta bitch.

"So, do you like it?"

Lying in bed buck naked, Floss hit the backwood filed with kush. Not one to really smoke, he did this night to relax and Tiffany's pink Victoria Secret panty and bra set was doing just that. "Yea, I like it. Come over here."

He watched as her bowlegs and thighs accentuated her body. Tiffany was stacked like a bookshelf. With her baby father in prison she kept her pussy nice, tight, and clean. Moving in his direction Tiffany climbed on top of the bed. Wasting no time she ran her hands up his bare leg as he inhaled and exhaled large plumes of smoke. When her lips wrapped around his pipe, he closed his eyes and enjoyed the warmth of her mouth.

Tiffany looked up at him and knew he liked it. Floss locked eyes with her as she slide her wet mouth up and down his dick. "That's it baby."

She felt him jump. "Oooh, I want this inside me."

"Okay, well do what cha do."

Climbing off the bed, Tiffany pulled down her panties and unclasped the bra. Floss sat up as she got back on the bed and laid her beneath him. Her skin was soft as he got between her legs. Wasting no time, he spread them and slid his dick all the way in. She was hot and ready lifting her hips to take all of him.

"Yes..."

He couldn't resist. Floss began to thrust, jabbing her hard as the bed rocked. Tiffany began to moan loud as he fucked the shit out of her. He knew she was infatuated with his mind and grind, and as long as he knocked her back in from time to time she would do any and everything he wanted.

Which is exactly what she did.

***

Months passed with him getting up to a half a brick from Big Don every two weeks. Tia was pissed because he stayed gone so long. But the day his son was born, he was by her side coming home every night. Just being in the hospital and seeing his son born changed him. But the streets still called for him, so he kept his grind one thousand percent. He woke up early one morning and received a call from his Uncle Smoke.

"Wassup Unc?"

"Man, the feds got Big Don."

He sat up quick, waking Tia. "What? When?"

"Listen, come outside. I'm out front, so we can talk."

Floss got up. "Alright, I'm on my way."

"Who's that baby?" Tia was worried. "Where you going?"

"That's my Uncle Smoke. The feds got Big Don. Smoke is outside right now," he explained.

Tossing on his jacket, Floss went out into the cold weather. The apartments they lived in were gated with a car port. As he followed the walkway, he saw a money green Ford Excursion with a custom grill, running in a parking spot. His uncle was in the driver's side waving him over.

"Damn Unc, this you?" said he asked as he got in. He saw 13-inch LCD flat screen DVD and six 7.5 TV's in every headset.

Closing the door Floss sat back. "So, when did they get him?"

"Late last night. He called me this morning."

His uncle explained that Big Don had been setup by this chick named Chrisy. She drove a milk white SC Lexus, buying coke from high rollers. Don and her had done business for over 10 years, that's how she got close to him.

"You know, Big Don just don't fool with anybody," he continued to say. "Word on the street is she got jammed up with a lot of bricks and now the feds are making her work it off by lining up major busts."

"Where this bitch live!" Foss was upset. "I'll go murk the bitch right now, today!"

But Smoke shook his head. "Nah man, Big Don knew you'd react like that. He told me to tell you to relax. He knows their expecting someone to try something like that. If she ends up hurt, they'll try to pin it on him."

"I'll make it look like an accident."

"For right now we'll chill, like I said."

The hurt and pain Floss felt was tremendous. Big Don had treated him like a little brother. With the absence of his father the OG gave him the guidance he needed to take his hustle to the next level.

Floss was in a daze. "So, what am I supposed to do now?"

"He told me to tell you to keep that money you owe him. He said be smart and stay on your feet." Smoke said. "I know you're fucked up, but he took a liking to you. All you can do now is be smart."

He knew the OG had the lawyer John Robinson on retainer. Floss spoke to the lawyer about his own issues and it was looking good for him getting the charges dropped. But he was sure Big Don's fate may be a little worse than his.

After telling his uncle to let him know when he ran across another plug on some good coke, Floss got out the truck. Big Don was now in jail and left him with $15,000 to add to the $8000 he already saved. Although shit was fucked up, Floss knew he couldn't let the OG down. Until he got word to handle the snitch, he would continue his grind.

But first he needed more coke.

***

Prince was a slick dude who stayed dressed like a playa. When Floss first met him, Prince was in Freetown, chilling at this stripper chick, Angel's, apartment. Rico-Suave knew Prince sold coke so when it came time Floss got at Angel, who setup the meeting.

Prince knew Floss was Big Don's younging so when he saw him sitting on Angel's couch, he felt comfortable. "What's up lil nigga? How's it been?"

Floss stood up and gave the dude some dap. Prince was only 6 years older than him, and cool as shit. "Honestly, things have been hard for the kid. The feds got the big homie and I'm hurtin' on a plug."

Prince looked at him for a brief minute, as if contemplating his thoughts. "Have you heard anything?"

"Yea. Some bitch Chrisy, in a milk white Lexus is workin'," he said. "So be careful."

"Hmph... yea, the bitch is workin'." Taking a seat, Prince
asked Angel to get him something to drink. She headed to
the kitchen. "So, what kind of work you lookin' for?" he
asked Floss.

"Look," he began. "I got two rollin' ass spots, movin'
half a brick every two weeks. And that's rock for rock."

"So, you need eighteen?"

He nodded. "And I got the cake. I got fifteen racks. All
I gotta do is go and get it and bring it wherever you want."

"Damn young nigga. You really have been on your shit,"
Prince said impressed. "But look, check this out... If you got
fifteen, how about I just shoot you a whole thang and you
give me the rest ASAP. That way we ain't gotta keep meetin'
every two weeks."

"What's the ticket on a brick?"

"I want twenty-seven-six. Can you handle that?"

The numbers were like a blessing to him. "Yea, fa sho."

With his new plug, Floss got back to work, hitting the
block like never before. He turned out every smokers' house
he knew. Before he wanted to be the man and serve weight.
Now he just cooked A1 straight drop crack and cut up everything in bigstones. He had Tiffany trapping for him along
with a few of his homeboys and another ride or die chick
named Neek.

All this hustling had Tia on one. She wanted things to
be different now that they had a child. She even tried to give
him a curfew; something he tried to respect at first but ended
up going against. There were clothes, food, and bills that
needed to be paid and he wasn't going to let his son want for
anything.

After eight weeks, Floss had more money than he ever expected. He was $60,000 strong. Between looking out for Big Don's needs, T-Roy's commissary, and mother, he helped to provide for his own family. His mother was getting worried which kept him on cue. Even as he rode through traffic or was in a trap house, he couldn't help but be paranoid. Seeing how Big Don got told on and still wondering if DC was still out there, possibly telling or plotting he kept one eye open.

As Floss sat in the parking lot on the Wendy's fast food restaurant, he tried not to look suspicious. He had $50,000 in a Nike book bag. Prince was bringing him 26 bricks and every car that rode by he kept his eyes on.

When the non-descript, pickup truck pulled into the parking lot at first Floss didn't see Prince behind the wheel. He was in Tiffany's whip since Prince knew the car. Pulling in next to him, Floss got out and jumped in the truck with the money. "It's all here," he said opening it so Prince could see the bundled rolls of rubber band money.

"Okay good," the man said. "We're gonna go through the drive thru. When you come back to your car the work will be on the front seat."

Following instructions, Floss just sat back while Prince drove thru. They ordered some food and after they pulled to the window and got the bags, Prince let him out. When he made it back to the whip, there was a green gym bag on the front seat. Floss got in and unzipped it.

Two solid bricks.

He started the car, looking in all three rear view mirrors. Despite his concerns, he was now knee deep in the game, wanting to do it big for Big Don. The OG and the streets needed him. And he wouldn't disappoint.

CHAPTER FIFTEEN

After getting a fiend to co-sign for him Floss was pushing a brand new black 97 Q-45 Infiniti on 22-inch wheels. Prince hated riding in it because he said it was too flashy, although he had his own fleet of fly cars. Floss bought it because he once told his old Four Horsemen crew that when he got his paper, he would cop an Infiniti Q-45.

He pulled into Levy Court and parked. Everybody was talking about him and he knew it. By applying himself with the principles Big Don gave him, he was coming up like a muthafucka. But he had gotten word that some didn't believe his rise was so honorable. A cat named Boodah from Annapolis had gotten robbed for over fifty stacks and some bricks of cocaine were taken from one of his stash spots while he was on vacation. Floss was told by his homeboy, Buddy, niggas was saying his name was in the mix and his new Q-45 gave them more reason to believe it.

Rico-Suave was serving fiends in the courtyard when he approached. "What's up? We're going to Dotson's tonight. It's my relative homegirl's birthday party."

He nodded. "Yea, I'm wit it."

Another one of their homeboys named Macho pulled up and parked. When he got out his Chevy 1500, he walked straight up to Floss. "Ayo, I just a call from Keon. He said that nigga Boodah and his people came through here last night, lookin' for you about that bullshit robbery he was told you were involved in."

Floss was getting tired of hearing his name thrown into something he had no involvement in. But to hear this nigga was coming into his neighborhood was something different. "Man get the fuck out of here! That nigga's comin' to Freetown? Call Keon."

"Hold up," Macho said dialing the number on his cell phone. When he got an answer he said, "Yo... Floss want to holler at 'chu."

Floss took the phone and spoke with Keon. Keon was from Annapolis and had known Floss for years. He was a young hustler himself. Even though there were beefing with cats from that city Keon never got involved in the foolishness, choosing money over everything. Floss hoped his partner could shed some light on this issue.

"Yea man, the nigga thinks you hit his spot," Keon said.

"But I don't know where this nigga lives or who he even is," Floss said. "I mean shit, I don't know what this nigga looks like!"

"Well he drives a black Range Rover. He's about twenty-two, light skinned and looks Chinese. That why we call him Boodah, really a cool nigga," Keon explained. "But he's got killas wit him ready to go. So be careful."

"Man fuck that nigga! I got killas too and if he ain't careful his ass can get aired out behind this shit. Keon, I came up off my grind. I don't need to rob nobody."

"I feel you. Just be on the lookout."

After Floss hung up, he was now informed that this Boodah situation was real could possibly turn ugly.

Later that night, Floss and his team headed to Dotson's to the birthday party. The spot was just around the corner from their hood, so they figured they'd swing over there to have a few drinks at the bar. When they arrived, the place was packed with people hanging in the parking lot and inside. Floss saw a lot of new faces, so he kept his eyes open.

"These niggas from everywhere," Snake said.

Rico Suave's female cousin was a bad ass little bitch and Floss knew if this was her home girls party there was no telling all the guys had they had invited.

"Aye look," Snake said nodding to a group of dudes chilling at the back of the establishment.

Floss saw cats from Annapolis, Glen Burnie, Mead Village, and Pioneer City all scattered about. The spot wasn't close to big enough to have all these different hoods in the building which could turn deadly in a matter of seconds. But as long as he had his .45, he just hoped nobody stepped to him wrong. For the most part, everyone looked to be having a good time, so he wasn't tripping.

After about an hour Floss and his crew were drinking and chilling by the bar. He needed this time to chill because he and Tia weren't seeing eye to eye. He was looking to take a little chick to the motel for the night since there was a bunch of them prancing around. Everywhere he looked he saw thick bitches and he had to have him one.

Now, Rico Suave's female cousin set all this up. Floss knew her because he had fucked her a few times. Up to that point he had been ducking her at the party. Her name was Silver and being she was a hell raise; Floss didn't need any messy bitches taking drama back to Tia.

He was about to approach this red bone chick at the bar when he heard Silver talking about him. "Yea fuck that nigga Floss," she said out loud. "Everybody know he is foul!" She was surrounded by a group of girls. As soon as he heard her, he turned and ran right up on her. She didn't see him coming so he startled her.

"What's up Silver? Why you over here wit my name in your mouth?" He knew she was really hating because he would not fuck her no more.

She was drunk. "Nigga, the streets got ya name in they mouth for robbing my man Boodah! That was some foul shit."

A few people heard her, and it was like the whole place went quiet, despite the music still playing. Floss said, "Bitch! What the fuck I look like robbin' a nigga? I got my own money. So, tell that nigga I said if he believes that shit, then he can see me any time!"

"Oh, he will nigga!" she said. "But that's what you get when you try to play me!" The way she said that made Floss wonder what she meant. But before he could even say another word, he saw a group of dudes congregated near him.

"Yea nigga!" Silver said. "Don't get scared now."

Turning, Floss saw the guys. Recognizing them to be from Annapolis, he said "What's up?"

A cat named Mike from the group approached them. "Are you alright, Silver?"

But Floss answered. "What if she ain't nigga?"

The guy gritted his teeth. "Nigga I wasn't talkin....."

Rico Suave interrupted by grabbing Silver by her arm. "Get'cho ass over here! Why you always startin' shit?"

"Nah cuz... this nigga...."

Before any other word escaped her mouth, Floss had upped his .45.

BOOM!! BOOM!!

The shots rang out scattering the people in the club in all four directions. Both hit Mike, dropping him to the ground.

With all the confusion surrounding his alleged involvement with Boodah, he wasn't taking any chances. Moving quickly Floss slid away from the crowd looking around for any of the guys with Mike. He saw them rushing out the front door. Quickly on their heels he didn't want them to beat him to the parking lot. If they did, he was sure to get trapped inside. When he made it out, he was surprised to find a clear path to his car.

"Yo Floss!"

Recognizing Buddy's voice, he turned in time to catch his homeboy running to his passenger's side. "Get in," he said.

"Man, what the fuck happened?"

Cars were pulling out of the parking lot left and right. Jumping behind the wheel Floss said, "That bitch Silver got these niggas thinking I robbed that nigga. I popped one of 'em and now I know for sure when I see that nigga Boodah imma have to put that gun to him too."

This was the first of many events to come, between Freetown and Boodah's crew from Annapolis. The word spread that Floss shot Mike behind Mike confronting him about robbing Boodah. Everyone twisted it and said Floss claimed he robbed Boodah behind him fucking Silver. But this was far from the truth and Floss knew she was the main one putting the rumor out there.

Now, with all the violence that spread, it made Freetown that much hotter with police. Prince was still supplying him with bricks and knew he was up to five every two weeks. Floss was up. But Tia's request for him to move out their apartment caused him and her to argue daily. In the end he found himself searching for a spot, finding one in Baltimore City.

With the success he was seeing and his newfound single life, Floss looked to have some fun.

***

Candy was a stripper chick that worked at the club Norma Jeans. She was 5'7, 140 pounds with the measurements of 28, 24, 41. She was light skinned, with long black hair, and green eyes. To Floss she resembled the singer Mya.

To break in his new bachelor pad, he called Candy to come chill. By the end of the night he had her buck-naked dancing for him. Floss enjoyed himself, taking his time with Candy. She had the best head, with full lips. He laid back and let her suck him into two nuts, before she put her hot and wet pussy on him.

"Do you like this pussy?" she asked.

It was good but he'd had tighter. "Yea, how 'bout this dick?" he shot back jabbing her deeply.

Candy's eyes rolled into the back of her head. With a constant jab, Floss hit her from the back. Her ass cheeks started clapping in rhythm of the bed squeaks.

"Yea.... Yea....shit!"

Cum boiled deep inside him as he unloaded causing her pussy to become extra slippery. Floss picked up his pace, trying to bring Candy into an intense climax.

He popped his thumb in her ass.

"Ahh...Ohhh...." She cried, biting the pillow then she clinched her eyes cumin' hard on his dick.

After fucking Candy that night, he figured he could use her, so he got at her about clients in the club. He knew she was a go getter and despite being a stripper she was really a D-girl at heart.

"I got a few niggas I know who be coppin' ounces of coke," she said. "Some of the girls be wanting grams for themselves."

"When's the next event you're doing?" he asked. Powder cliental would mean he wouldn't have to cook it.

"Tomorrow night at VFW. If you want, I can take a few bags with me,"

"That'll be cool," he told her. "But I wanna come too. Tell any of your homeboys if they're trynah get right, come thru."

Candy said she would.

When that night came around Floss hit VFW's deep. His homeboys Rockey, Jake the Snake, Rico Suave, Buddy, Rusty, and about 10 more all went. His plan was to tap into the club scene because if he had the block also that would be more money. Pushing the Infiniti Floss, he pulled into the parking lot and saw all the cars. Something told him there was going to be some shit; VFWs were live. As soon as Floss entered, he saw people enjoying themselves, partying hard. The DJ was at the booth with two bad bitches. It seemed everybody came out.

"Aye, Floss," Rusty said tapping him on the shoulder. "Look"

As soon as he turned his head Floss saw a little bit of every hood in there, including Annapolis dudes. The beef was still alive, so he was definitely going to keep his eyes peeled. "Man, we're here to have a good time, and see about this money. If niggas get to trippin' then it's on."

Ever since he shot Mike the streets was buzzing about the dudes people looking for him. Fortunately, Mike survived, barley getting up off life support hours earlier. Candy found him chilling at a table with his crew. She had sold a few grams and introduced him to a few dudes looking to score a couple ounces. That's when the fight broke out. Not wanting to get caught in the mix, Floss and his boys jumped as dudes and females started running for the doors. Rico Suave led the way as a crew of Annapolis cats came towards them.

"Get that nigga!" was all he heard.

When Floss looked, he saw a gun pointed at him. He ducked.

BOOM!! BOOM!!

He heard a scream as he scattered outside. A few more shots and bullets whizzed by. Moving with the crowd he dashed to his car and jumped inside. Rusty was right on his heels, leaping in the passenger's side. Jake the Snake and Buddy jumped in the back.

BOOM!! BOOM!!

"Nigga roll out!!" Buddy yelled.

Floss started the car and dropping it in gear he smashed out the parking lot, almost running over a few people. What he'd come to find out was the last two bullets aimed at his truck, struck and hit Jack the Snake. His brains were all over the backseat. A loss he would carry forever.

CHAPTER SIXTEEN

Back at the federal facility......Present Day

M iles was stuck. He couldn't believe his ears. "That nigga Boodah next door? He's the one you were beefin' wit?"

Floss nodded. "Yep. All behind silver's lyin' ass. But the tripped-out part is, me and him only seen each other personally one time. And that was at a fight in Glen Burnie."

"How'd you know it was him?"

"He knew my car and I knew his Range Rover." Floss got up from the bunk and walked to the cell door. "It came out Silver was lyin' about me robbin' his spot when his ex-bitches brother admitted to plotting it altogether."

"Damn that's fucked up. So, Silver tossed your name in there trynah get back at you?" He nodded. "Yea and got some good men killed."

Mail call was being conducted and Floss heard the officer call the light skinned Muslim dudes name from Annapolis.

"Inmate Mitchell!"

"Here I go," the guy replied.

Floss stepped from the door. "Somethin' about that nigga don't add up."

"Who, that sunni-nigga?"

"Yea, but it will come to light."

Since his lawyer came to visit him, Floss had been on the phone heavy. Talking in code he called Tia and a few of his homeboys, he put the word out about the informant on his case. It took a few weeks but finally the name Andrew Stewart popped up. Tia came to visit, giving him an update.

"Rusty and them found dude," she said. "It was a white boy with gold teeth. Ring a bell?"

At first, he didn't recall but then it hit him. "Yea. So, what was the outcome?"

She gave him a look that said it all. "Let's just say he's no longer with us."

When he got back to the unit, Floss told Miles about it. "One day one of my friends called me saying they had a cat that they'd been dealing with for a while. They were looking to score nine ounces," he said thinking back. "I met them both at Pete's Cycle, the shopping center. When I got there the fiend was with this white boy. He had cornrows and gold teeth."

Miles said, "Gold teeth? Where the fuck was he from?"

"Florida, I think."

Floss went on to explain how when he got there everything was cool. He jumped in his car and jumped in the Crown Vic with the fiend and white boy. The car was decked out on 20-inch Ashanti rims, candy painted dark blue with white leather interior. He could tell the white boy was getting money and paid the $8,200 amount with no problem.

"He went by the name Whiteboy," he continued. "I dealt with him a few times. He was getting money out in Aberdeen, Maryland."

"I bet he got busted and that's how he ended up jumpin' on your case," Miles said. "How'd they find him?"

"Tia said her home girl Sasha recognized the name. When they realized it was him, she told a few of my homeboys. They took it from there."

"She said they killed him?"

He nodded. "Yea. He's a goner."

Miles smiled. "Well shit, that's one down!"

But Floss was not satisfied. "Yea, but there's still one more mu'fucka out there. And I got a trial in thirty days. If I don't find 'em soon, shit can get ugly for me."

The news of Andrew Stewart's death spread quickly and Mr. Ravenell was up there with an update days after.

"Although this situation was unfortunate for him, this helps your case a little," the lawyer said. "At least on the drug charges. We still have the other person testifying against you."

Floss shook his head. "How can I defend myself if I don't know who's testifying? I pay you to defend me so I need that name!"

"Listen Mr. Blacksmith...."

"No! You listen." He was upset beyond measure. "I gave you forty thousand dollars! Find out who's testifying so we can prepare a defense. We got one month before trial, and I'm not gonna let some snitch set me up because they're in a fucked-up situation with these people."

Mr. Ravenell got the message clear as day. "Okay, I'm on it."

"I hope so because I don't wanna see you again unless you got that name." Once he said this he jumped up and beat on the door for the officer to come get him.

"I'll see you soon," his lawyer said.

Floss never looked back.

When Floss got back to the unit his head was hurting so bad that he had to lay down. From the beginning of all this, his only goal was to get some money and get out the game.

Unlike many he knew, who got long runs, he wasn't given that luxury. But as long as he had cats on the streets who still had genuine love for him, he knew he could get past all this. It was just going to take time. Something he did not have.

Days passed by and being locked up in county was becoming like hell to him. Floss spent his days blowing up everybody's phone, either talking shit or getting the latest updates on what was going on in Freetown. Until his lawyer found out the name of the other informant, he couldn't do anything which caused him to stress. So, the phone and chopping it up with his cellie was his only relief.

"So, how's your case lookin'?" He asked changing the subject.

Miles exhaled and shook his head. "My lawyer is supposed to be up here this week", he said." Their offering all this time, but ain't got no evidence. I'm trynah stall to see if they come up with a better deal."

Floss knew Miles' back was against a wall. Although he knew his cellie was a gangsta, Miles wasn't trying to do all that time. But he couldn't blame the man for fighting.

"So, tell me this," Miles began. "Whatever happened to Big Don?"

"They gave the big homie thirty years for the Rico Act. That shit fucked me up too because the bitch Chrissy, who set him up, was still out there," he said. "I swear I was spooked."

"Nobody tried to find her ass?"

He nodded. "Yea, but she relocated after that."

Floss told him how the whole city became wide open with cats from all over trying to capitalize off their drug market; the murder rate went up quick. However, Freetown remained untouched as word spread fast that they weren't having no new niggas posting up in their hood.

"After the towers got hit by those planes in New York, coke prices went up," he explained. "My boy prince's people couldn't keep up with the supply, so I found a new plug on some good coke."

"Oh Yea?" Miles replied with peeked interest.

"Yea. But I almost missed it at first because of the nigga."

Miles frowned. "Why? What was wrong with him?"

Floss broke down how he had a partner named red. After 911 red began plugging with small quantities of coke just to get by. Overtime Floss asked the man to allow him to add some money with his, so when he re-upped, he could get it too.

"Red was a cool nigga and said I could," he said. "So, I gave him eighty-thousand for three bricks. After a couple times his people wanted to meet me. It turned out to be this nigga named Zeek. And at first, me and this nigga didn't click."

Whenever Floss would meet Red and Zeek he was told not to bring anyone. But Zeek would have a couple niggas with him. This pissed Floss off. He was also searched a few times. Although it irritated him, Floss kept his cool because the coke was always good, and he really needed it because there was no steady flow of coke in his hood.

"Zeek didn't trust nobody," he said. "Not even Red for real."

Miles laughed. "Niggas be like that tho?"

"Yea, but that shit had me ready to murk his ass. I've never been that type of nigga who bit the hand that fed him."

"How did things turn out in the end?"

"Shit as he got to know me, he opened up. He saw I was about my money so all the rumors about my homeboys and the shootouts eventually stopped playing a role in his mind," he said. "Because that's what had him spooked to deal with me from the jump."

"Damn," Miles said thinking. "You were getting paid! Why didn't you invest in something?"

"I did," he said. "But I'll tell you about that later. Right now, let me use this phone. I gotta call Tia."

Floss stepped out the cell and a cat named Roscoe from Baltimore was standing near the slider waving for him. Roscoe was from the Latrobe projects.

"Ayo, Boodah's callin' for you.", Roscoe told him.

He made his way over. "Good lookin' out."

Roscoe stepped away and he pounded the door twice. *Boom! Boom!*

Seconds later, he heard Boodah's muffled voice. "Floss is that you?"

"Yea, what's up?"

"Man, I just came back from my lawyer's visit. You know I go to court next week."

He did know Boodah was about to start trial. He was keeping up with it like it was his own. "So, what's he sayin?"

"If I don't do something quick about these rats, it's lookin' bad for me, yo. The main informant to my drug conspiracy is the key and I can't find his bitch ass." Boodah replied with frustration in his voice.

"What about all those other people?" He asked remembering the long list of names.

"Most of them have been discredited or my lawyer feels they don't have any real information for the government to use," Boodah revealed. "The main nigga who's snitchin' is saying he bought nine ounces from me every week for two years. He's saying I supplied him and two more niggas in his crew."

Floss knew how the feds worked. They would add each transaction up into one large drug amount. Boodah's meant he'd be accountable for selling one kilo a month for 24 months, equaling 24 kilograms of cocaine. It would trigger an automatic life sentence.

"Who in the fuck is this nigga?"

"Well we call him Lucky," Boodah said. "But his real name is Devon Mitchell. He is from my city and I've called everywhere but nobody can seem to find the nigga. If I find him, I got some action."

As soon as Boodah mentioned the name, an alarm went off in his head. Floss could not figure out why, but the name rang a bell. "Devon Mitchell? Yea, I remember seeing that name on your paper."

"Yea, tall yellow nigga... You've probably seen that nigga out there in the city." Floss began looking around the unit as he thought. His mind raced trying to put together the dots. Something seemed odd and he could not put his finger on it. Then it hit him. "Hey you remember that nigga I asked you about, who's over here with me?"

"Who the Muslim nigga? Abdullah...some shit?"

"Yea."

"What about him?" Then before Floss could respond Boodah said. "Oooh, what he look like?"

"He's about six-three, slim, light skinned with waves and big ass beard on his face."

A brief silence. "Nah, that nigga Lucky ain't got no beard."

"Man, a nigga can grow a beard like it ain't shit. I'm just askin' because this nigga be actin' all funny and plus I heard the C.O. call his name for mail call."

"What is it?"

"Mitchell," he replied.

Boodah could not believe the coincidence. "For real?"

"Yep. So, what's the odds?"

"Okay, tell me this? Does he have tattoos?"

He could not remember seeing any on the man. He was trying to locate him in the unit but he was nowhere to be found. "I'm not sure. I haven't really seen...."

As soon as he spoke the guy in question exited his cell and made his way over to use the phone, which was several feet away from him. Now he had a good look at him. Lowering his voice, Floss said, "Hold up he's right here."

The man turned to look at Floss. Then, dropping his eyes, he turned his back to him as he dialed numbers on the phone. With his arms exposed Floss was able to see tattoos clearly.

Lowering his voice, he said, "Hey..."

"Yea..." Boodah replied in a whisper also.

"He got some."

"Do you see a cross on his forearm and tattoo tears on his face?"

Floss saw both. Smiling he said, "He's got both. I'm telling you it's him. But there's only one way to really be sure."

"How?"

Taking a chance, Floss simply called out the guy's name. "Aye Lucky!"

And like magic the man turned and faced him. The look on his face told the whole story. Floss had found the man responsible for Boodah's whole indictment.

CHAPTER SEVENTEEN

When Floss saw the look on the man's face, he knew he had him. Not wanting to tip him off he smiled and looked away, talking into the crack of the slider and switching up his approach.

"Lucky? Man, if you went and got three years, you're not lucky! You're blessed!" he said laughing.

He cut his eyes and saw the Muslim cat at the phone still looking at him. A confused and suspicious expression was on his face, but then finally he figured it was nothing and returned to his call.

Boodah asked through the door. "Ayo, Floss what was that?"

His voice was low. Turning his back to the phones Floss said, "yeah, it's him.

"What? Ayo, that bitch ass nigga!" Boodah was livid. "Man, call that nigga to the slider so I can holler at him."

"For what? Ayo, there's only one way to handle a rat."

"But how am I gonna get to him?"

With all the frustration he was feeling Floss said, "Look, let me take care of it."

"Are you sure?" the sound in Boodah's voice was etched with confusion.

"Yeah, just chill," he said. "We still got a few weeks before you go to trial. That gives us enough time to bake this nigga a cake."

On cue the voice of the officer working the control booth came booming over the loudspeaker. "Inmate step away from the slider!"

Floss said, "My nigga, I'll holla...."

"Fa'sho," Boodah replied. And much love.

He couldn't believe the turn of events. While trying to figure out his own issues with snitches he managed to find the person testifying on another cat. To think the feds would try to hide a person right next door to the person they were telling on was amazing. But Floss felt himself to be a real nigga. Even though he and Boodah had a history, all that was behind them now. They were both in the same position and the rules to the game still had to be abided. He knew what he had to do.

Miles could not believe his ears when Floss revealed who Boodah's snitch was. "I knew that weird ass nigga was suspect!" he said shaking his head. "So, what do you wanna do?"

Pacing back and forth in his cell, Floss thought about the situation carefully. "Well I've already made my mind up to punish the nigga. But because Boodah still has some time before he goes to trial, I wanna line up a few things myself in case I go to the hole."

With firm aggression, his cellie objected. "Nah, in case WE go to the hole! Nigga, I'm ridin' if you're goin' too."

He nodded his head. Since he was transferred to Talbert County, him and Miles had gotten close. They shared almost everything. Floss knew the man didn't really have family, and for that he tried to show Miles how much he appreciated his loyalty.

"Okay look.... if we can somehow convince this nigga not to testify, without smashing him, then that's what I wanna do."

"How do you plan on doin' that?"

"Easy!" he replied. "Whoever he keeps callin', whoever keeps sending him letters, money and is visiting him... Whoever that is, I'm gonna find out. With that as a bargaining chip, he may fold."

Miles got the picture. "So, threaten to kill them if he testifies?"

"Exactly."

"And if that doesn't work?"

Floss shook his head. "Shit, we'll just stomp his head into the ground until it splits like a melon. Fuck that rat ass nigga, straight up."

***

Days passed by and like usual the unit was quiet. Guys were going to court almost every other day. Floss noticed the snitch nigga, Lucky, was leaving out on lawyer's visit sometimes twice a day. When he would return, he would have a suspicious look in his eyes, always darting to the phone. One time Floss used the phone next to him and overheard a conversation he was having with some chick. Upon closer inspection he realized the female was his baby mother.

Being patient Floss found out more when he went to visit. In the booth with Tia, he saw lucky with a light skinned chick and an older lady, he assumed was his or her mother. They had two small boys no older than four and five years old. "That's the nigga right there," he told Tia. He mentioned Lucky before, so now he gave her the face of the man.

She looked and said, "Yeah I've seen her up here a few times. We've spoken. That's her man. He was in another unit before they moved him over here with you."

"Do me a favour," he began. "Follow them when you leave. Pass the address off to the homies."

He did not like getting Tia involved. But since her dealings with the last issue with killing the white boy she seemed willing. Having her pass the info to Buddy, Rusty, and Rico suave meant it would get handled. There was no way he could see this snitch win, trying to throw Boodah under the bus, regardless of old beef.

In the meantime, Mr. Ravenell was coming through more, giving updates. He finally received the name of the other individual testifying against him, and like suspected it was another cat who had gotten caught up in a case.

"His name is Dexter Colbert. He's currently being held in the super max institution downtown for conspiracy to distribute cocaine in the state of Maryland and three weapon charges and attempted murder in DC."

As soon as Floss heard the name, he knew exactly who it was, DC.

"You look like you know this guy?" Removing his glasses Mr. Ravenell said, "Listen I don't know what happened to the other guys. But this informant is incarcerated, which means their holding him until he rolls on you. So I'm going to need you to tell me everything I need to know in order to help you."

Floss wasn't very thrilled about admitting everything, even if it was his lawyer. Not until he figured out what dc was alleging, he did. "Yeah, I know this fool. But I haven't seen him in two years. Back then we were hustling crumbs."

"Well, that's not what he's alleging. He saying he has information about murders, drug deals, and the workings of an enterprise. And he's saying you're the head of this organization."

Floss just laughed.

"Listen, this is no laughing matter. If....."

He cut his lawyer off. "I know this isn't a laughing matter. I'm the one in jail."

"Then what do you want me to do?"

"Just find out what unit he's in and I'll do the rest," he said.

That night he was sitting in his cell. Miles was on the top bunk leaning on his elbow.

Both were trying to figure out what Floss' next move should be.

"So," Miles began. "You don't know anybody who works there. Nobody you know is in jail there?"

He shook his head. "Not that I know of."

"Damn because if there was then you could get them on his ass."

"I know, but I got about a month still, so that's enough time to figure it out." Floss got up off his bunk and looked out the cell door. He saw Lucky on the phone. "Until then, what you think about this nigga?"

"I think we should holler at him tonight," Miles replied matter of fact.

When he got back from his lawyer's visit, Floss called Tia, who told him she gave Lucky's mother and girlfriend addresses to the homies. After following them she found out they stayed only minutes away from the jail. Seeing no reason to waste time he said, "Fuck it. Let me call my boy. If he says he got time to handle it, we will."

Floss' plan was to have Rusty slide by the address. He chose him because Rusty had no conscious. After several tries, he managed to reach his homeboy, finding him already in traffic.

"I just left this little bitch spot, gettin' some head," he told Floss. "So yeah, I'll slide by there."

"Cool, I'll give you twenty minutes. Then I'mma get on this nigga top. He'll hit them soon after."

"Fa sho."

With that in place the last part was to approach Lucky. So, once he was off the phone both him and Miles fell up in the man's cell catching him right after his evening prayer. When he opened his cell door and stepped in uninvited, it almost scared the shit out of Lucky.

"What's up man?" Floss asked. "Do you mind if we come in?"

"I uhh....."

"What did you say your name was?" Miles asked next.

A mixed expression was on his face. "My name is Abdullah Rasool....." "He began with an Arabic accent.

"Nigga cut it out," Floss interrupted. "Your name is Lucky, right?"

At that moment the man knew that his cover was blow. He grew defensive. "Look my name is Abdullah Rasool Muhamed. I don't go by my street name anymore. Not since I gave my life to Allah."

Floss laughed. As he approached Lucky, the slim man began to back up, especially when Miles blocked off the other side. "Nigga you funny. You mean ever since you started snitchin',"

Moving fast Lucky tried to bolt for the door but Floss was too quick. Throwing a hook, he caught the man across the jaw, dropping him into the small metal desk. As he flailed his arms Miles grabbed him in a full nelson, making it to where he could not move and standing him up straight. Miles was way stronger than the frail man.

Floss pointed a finger in his face. Gritting his teeth, he spoke with steel in his eyes. "Now listen you bitch. I got my man at your baby mama's and mother's house right now, ready to murk them and your sons. I want you to call them, so you know I ain't playin'. If for any reason you try to call the C.O., he'll kill 'em. You hear me?"

Lucky got quiet and quit struggling and listened. When he realized Floss was not playing, he said, "What do you want me to do?"

Simply, Floss said "You testifying on Boodah. I want you to retract your story.

Whatever deal you were trying to get, that's over. Do that and your family stays safe."

"Boodah... Who's Boodah?"

WHAM!!!

The moment his fist made contract to Lucky's face the man's head snapped back like a punching bag. Instantly, his lip busted, and his mouth began to bleed really bad. "Nigga! You actin' like you don't know what I'm talking about will only get them killed."

"Okay... Okay... Okay...." Lucky got some straightening about himself.

"Now nigga," Floss said. "Go make that call, if you think I'm playin'."

Miles flung him towards the door, causing a loud thud. "Go!"

Despite his mouth bleeding and looking roughed up, Lucky headed straight to the phone. There was panic and concern on his face as he dialed the numbers. Floss stood and watched as the man's facial expressions turned to fear as he spoke to someone on the other end of the line. After giving patient orders he hung up the phone looking afraid. That's when he headed back to the cell.

"Okay. I'll do it." Lucky said quietly.

Floss knew rusty must have scared the shit out of Lucky's people. And from the looks of it he did a good job handling business. "And if you do, I'll keep my promise."

"But you said that was it."

"It is," he replied. "But if you try to switch units the deal is off. I wanna keep an eye on your ass. And remember, if for some reason i can't call my boy, or even if I'm late, that could cost your family their lives."

Lucky thought about the terms. Being a known informant in the unit did not seem so appealing.

"And don't worry, nobody will fuck with you," Floss assured him. "Just do your part."

With the deal in place, Floss felt good that the whole situation was now under control. Come to find out Lucky was only facing eight years in federal prison. With guidance him and Miles convinced Lucky that it was best he did not snitch, and to do his time like a man. Floss did everything to keep the man off the stand; everything he could.

When the time finally rolled around for Boodah to start trial it was looking good. His lawyer relayed the good news about the key informant not willing to testify, which left the whole case weak. The day of trial, Boodah came back to the jail with the best news Floss had heard his whole time there.

"They threw it out!" he yelled through the slider. "I'm going home today and it's all because of you!"

Floss was smiling ear to ear. "Nah man, I just did what any real nigga would've done. That's all."

But Boodah felt different. "On some real shit... Dog, after all the shit we went through. Man, I owe you the world.

And I promise, whatever you need I got' chu. Straight up! You name it."

This gave him the best feeling.

"Maybe... One day. I'll let you know."

Boodah's release came as big news to the streets. When Floss called everybody was talking about it. Even though he was happy for the man, he wished he could solve his own issues with rats and the feds. So, he could finally return to the streets himself.

CHAPTER EIGHTEEN

F loss still had three weeks until his trial started. He worked hard on the phones, three-waying cats he knew and seeing Tia on visits talking about finding someone to get to DC. His mother told him T-Roy got out of prison finally and was grateful for the money he left him.

"He's staying at his grandmother's house," she told him. "His mother had been stressing, afraid for him."

Floss looked at her and said, "I'll call him tonight. How about you? Are you okay?"

Exhaling a long sigh, she titled her head to the side and with loving eyes she smiled. "I'll never be alright with you in here baby. But I understand that you gotta live your life."

He nodded. "What's up with pops?"

"He's cool. Says he loves you. Your grandma says you'll be home soon, so that's why she won't come up here."

Floss smiled. "That's right tell her I said keep prayin'."

For a whole hour his mother updated him on the happenings in the streets. She said Big Don called and told him to take whatever deal the government offered. The crackhead, Pops, died of a heart attack, from getting high during sexual acts. His homeboy, Buddy, moved to Elizabeth, New Jersey because his name came up by the feds; things were still hectic.

When he got back to the unit Floss called T-Roy grand-mother's house to holler at his partner.

"Wussup!" T-Roy voice was full of excitement. "I heard you had it turnt up out here." He laughed. All the time T-Roy was locked up Floss kept money on his books and spoke to him regularly. But now T-Roy was able to see it for himself.

"I told you nigga. How you like the whip?"

"Man, that bitch is fly! Nigga, i got out pushin' a Q-Fo-finite! My ex-bitch lookin' real stupid right now!"

The Q45 infinity was the first car Floss bought. After that he copped a Jaguar XK8 drop-top, leaving the Q45 at T-Roy grandmother's house for when he got out. "Yea I wanted you to get out on the right foot, or should I say four wheels."

"Fa sho," T-Roy replied. "But anyway, what's it lookin' like for your situation?"

Floss broke down how the feds had no case and now dc was snitching, to get out of his own issues. Not getting too graphic over the phone, he kept it simple and told him he had it all handled. "Right now you just worry about g'tting' back right," he told T-Roy. "And be careful, them niggas is workin' wit them folks. You see how they had Boodah."

"Ayo, I was going to tell you, I saw him the other day at Townson Town Center Mall. He told me to give him a call he had something for me. Ya'll got cool like that?"

"Yeah, call him up. They say he's doing good."

"He is," T-Roy said. "The nigga jumped out a two door all white Benz, shining like a light bulb. The boy had dia-monds everywhere."

Floss had gotten word Boodah was back on in the game. "But look, if everything goes right, I'll be back out there soon. I just need you to keep yourself out of trouble. Can you do that?"

T-Roy laughed. "Yeah. I can do that."

"Oh," he said. "who do you know that's locked up at super max?"

"I can't think of anybody. But if I find out I'll let you know. Call me back tonight." Floss hung up the phone and headed over to the table where Miles sat watching TV. Lucky was still in their unit, keeping himself regulated to his cell most of the time. After he received the time he signed for he was simply waiting to pull chains and leave the jail.

"Damn man, I need to find someone at that jail. I'll pay fifty-grand for someone to off that nigga DC"

Miles looked around suspiciously. "Aye, let's go to the cell," he said. "We don't need to be talking like this in the unit."

Floss knew he was right. He had a lot on his mind and didn't feel like being out there anyway. So, the two of them went to the cell, where he gave Miles a run down about things.

"So ya boy got out?" Miles asked.

"Yea. He's out there stuntin' on his ex-bitch in the whip I left him, so she's all fucked up he got right out doing his thing."

Miles shook his head. "Damn nigga, you really came along way. Even after big don got locked up, you got wit' prince and then red and continued to get it."

He nodded. "I had to. My mom was struggling' with my little brother and sister and my uncles always needed help." Floss sat on his bunk. "Then when me and Tia split it seemed like I was paying for separate households. Mine and hers."

"Well that's cool you were able to look out for your boy."

"That's what we do it for," he said. "To look out for self, real niggas and family." Miles asked, "So what did you get into, on the legit side? You said you started investing money. How?"

"Do you remember my boy Diddy, the bails-bondsman?"

"The one you got to get T-Roy out that time?"

He nodded. "Yeah. Come to find out, Diddy had been in the dope game for years. After I used him when i got locked up, me and him got real cool. Plus, big don called him and put in a good word about me."

"What type of shit did you invest in?"

Instead of giving a quick response. Floss stayed true to his pattern and broke the whole story down. This is what they did, with all the time on their hands. It was not like either were going anywhere anytime soon.

CHAPTER NINETEEN

The year 2000

Floss' money was coming in good. He had Key, Tiffany, and several of his homeboys trappin' for him. At 20 years old he was riding clean and everyone knew Freetown was getting money, and not to be fucked with. His crew popped pistols and bottles, getting respect from many.

One day he ran into Diddy. The bondsman asked him what he was doing with all the money he was getting in the streets. Floss had no real answer saying he knew he needed to do something instead of stack it for a rainy day.

"Well, I got a partner who can invest in real estate for you," Diddy explained.

Floss was confused. "Why.... I don't understand?"

"He can clean it up. You see, he can buy and sell the houses and you'll even make a profit."

Diddy went on to explain the fix-it and flip it game to him. He told Floss the amounts of money he could make, and how he'd been doing it himself. "i started the bail bonds company off dope money. Now I'm getting the best of both worlds. Legit and street money."

When he got a call from Big Don he asked him for his opinion. The OG told him he could trust Diddy.

"I recommend you do it," Big Don advised. "The streets will turn but being legit will keep your money straight for the long run."

Floss hit Diddy the day after talking to big don and told him he wanted to meet his partner. Diddy said he would line it up but wanted him to go look at a building with him.

"What are you lookin' at a building for? Are you about to open up another location for the bonds service?"

"Yeah," Diddy said. "I'll break it all down when we get there. You need to see this side of the game and I promised big don I'd turn you on to it."

Floss met Diddy at his office and the two rolled in Diddy's Chrysler 300. As they rolled through the city, the man opened his mind to all the things he could be doing with his money. When they got to the building Diddy met with some white man and closed the deal on leasing it.

"Fuck it." Floss began as they sat at a small Mexican restaurant eating lunch. "How about I go in with you on this new spot you're going to open?" It only made sense, seeing all the legit money Diddy was making.

Diddy laughed. "Are you serious?"

"Hell yeah. I got the cake. We can call it best of both world's bonds-men."

Now Diddy was really laughing. "You think you're ready for this?"

Floss tossed his hands up. "Who is ever ready? All I know is to go get it. And I see how many niggas we know need bond, let alone the others gettin' locked up so I can see the money."

That day Floss and Diddy became partners, leaving the youngster feeling like a changed man. He was up in the morning well dressed and out his door heading to his new job, being a company man. At night he was in the trap-spot either whipping the work, dropping it or picking up the money, truly the best of both worlds.

Diddy showed his hand to the dope game early. Floss arrived at work early, like usual, and the man was in the back of their newly renovated office weighing a few bricks.

"How much you gettin' them for?" he asked.

"Twenty-nine," Diddy replied. "Usually I have my man Rodney handle this shit. But he's out of town so I'm puttin' it together."

Floss knew Rodney and Diddy had a clothing store together. He was beginning to see how a lot of cats who owned small businesses had their hand in the street game. "Oh yeah, my boy said he found a spot we can put some money into. Are you still interested?"

"How much?" he asked. His mind began to race, adding up how much bread he had saved.

Diddy said, "Whatever you want to invest. Ten, twenty it's on you."

"Where is the house?"

"B-More." Diddy replied." We can go check it out together, this weekend."

Willing to look deeper, Floss went and saw the three bedroom 1 1/2 bath one story crib. He decided to give $40,000 to Diddy and the two move in and fixed the spot up in less than 3 months.

The next venture Diddy brought was investing in a music studio. He knew a cat who built them for the low and after furnishing it with all the equipment they would sell studio time to all the local artists. Floss loved the idea.

All of the extra activities took Floss out of the street life. He was not hanging in Freetown and at the strip clubs like he used to. This proved to be good for him. Cats were getting locked up left and right, so he stayed out the way.

Since he got her the apartment Tia had begun taking her newfound freedom and was becoming more independent of him. She had gotten a job at child day care and was making good money. But every now and then they would go out and have lunch. No matter what Floss knew Tia was down and had been, since the night he took her virginity.

Sitting across from him, Tia smiled as she sipped her soda. "You really surprised me." she said.

"Surprised you like how?" Floss felt relaxed in the far corner of the restaurant.

"You've been dressing better, doing your business stuff and stayin' away from the street corners."

He laughed. "I was never no street corner nigga, from the jump. I trap out of spots. Ain't no nigga gon' ride by and pop me, because I'm eatin'."

She just shook her head. "Anyway, we're gonna change the subject cuz i wanna have a serious conversation with you."

"What's up? Is everything cool?"

Tia nodded. "Yeah, I just wanted to ask how you felt about us movin' back in together." the words were hard for her to say. "Our son asking about you all the time really hurts. And I'm tired of being by myself."

For the past few weeks he had been playing with her, saying how he changed. He actually asked her this same thing. Now he felt it was the right time to get his girl and son back with him. "I mean that's all I want," he said. "When you ready, today?" she just laughed. "You just want some pussy boy."

He smiled. "You know it. In house pussy is the best, especially yours."

Tia's concerns about him partying and staying out were her main issues. He promised to behave and get himself to the point where he would finally be done with the drug game altogether. In the meantime, Floss told himself he was going to grind harder than ever to achieve his goal quicker.

The situation with red plugging him with Zeek was starting to get better. He realized Zeek wanted him to come alone so he could get to know him. The two dudes he kept were just protecting the work. Floss found out that Zeek was really connected to a source out of Miami so everybody was being watched.

Just like all good things, some bullshit came when Zeek got busted. He called the bond service to get Floss and Diddy to bail him out. The cost was one million dollars.

"I got 'chu Floss.... Do this for me and I got chu." he said in a pleading tone.

Diddy was not so optimistic. "Listen, here's where you gotta use your gut feeling. On one hand he's plugged in but on the other hand he may disappear."

Floss had a good feeling. "I think we should do it."

Despite all that, the bail was reduced soon after to $100,000. After 72 hours, Zeek was released and in front of them by himself.

"That nigga red snitched on me; straight forward.

Floss could not believe his ears. "What!"

Zeek shook his head. "I know... I know... And i just want you to know I never once thought you knew anything."

"I didn't! Man, where that bitch ass nigga?" Floss asked emphatically.

"My people are lookin' now," Zeek said. "But look, you helped me and now I'm gonna help you. For you helping me, I've arranged for you to get ten bricks every time regardless of how much money you got. All of em' at eighteen a piece."

So, it seemed reds betrayal turned into his opportunity. With this Floss began his newfound mission, to grind and go legit, on a good foot. Zeek's lawyer passed off court dates

and staying low-key allowed Floss to do his thing on a major level. Freetown had a new Big Don and his name was Floss.
Everybody loved it.
Well, everyone but Tia.

CHAPTER TWENTY

Zeek stayed true to his promise. Floss kept work 247 and soon he was serving whole bricks to cats he really fucked with.

Taking a few of his homeboys, Floss took Zeek's advice and went to Baltimore for the auto showcase. Zeek knew a guy who could hook them up with whatever car they wished. Floss had his mind set on a Benz or Escalade. If he could get both, then he would.

The place was located on Reisterstown Road and North Parkway. When Floss, Rico-Suave, and Buddy arrived it was busy with people. The place was a small car lot filled with all high-end luxury vehicles. It had every car that a D-boy ever wanted; big cars sitting on big wheels.

"Damn, they ain't got the Escalade," Floss said. He was hoping they did.

Earlier he called the Gary, the guy Zeek connected him with. When a white dealer approached them, Floss saw he was indeed his man.

"May I help you?"

He smiled. "Yeah, my boy Zeek sent me."

"Oh yeah, Zeek," the man replied smiling. "Of course. You see anything you like?"

An all-white 2001 Mercedes Benz S500 sitting on 22-inch Luxor rims called his name from the far corner. "Yea, wussup wit that 'cedes? And do yall got an Escalade EXT?"

It was right then and there that Gary knew he had another great customer. "The Mercedes is just for you. And the escalade... We'll talk more about ordering one if you'd like."

Floss smiled. "Yeah, let's talk about it."

Hitting the city of Pasadena at 21 with a brand-new Benz upped his level in the game. Now niggas knew he was on, and not just some cat who came up off his pop's name. He now was his own man. Floss celebrated his new whip by going to the strip club. And as soon as he stepped in the spot all the bitches were on his dick.

Literally.

When Candy asked him if she could give him some head, Floss slid out, leaving his homeboys. The whole night they poured up bottles while strippers gave them one on one strip teases. So, his dick was hard as fuck.

"Ain't nothing like a bad bitch with some bomb head," he whispered as his toes curled. Candy was slapped his hard wood across her face, before swallowing him deep into her mouth.

"You like that?" she asked as her tongue played with the underside of his dick, sending a sensation through his body.

"Here it comes."

Floss arched his hips, driving his dick deeper into her throat. Then like a blast his nut shot in her mouth as her lips tightened around his shaft. She rolled his nut sack between her fingers, intensifying the feeling.

"Mmmmm..." She cooed.

That's when the two back doors burst open. It was Buddy and this other stripper names Juicey.

"Ohhh, naw yall ain't," Juicey said smiling. She saw her homegirl doing her thang to Floss.

"Damn nigga," Floss said as he watched Buddy getting comfortable.

Pulling down his pants, Buddy spread his legs as Juicey went to work on his joint.

"That's right girl," he said exhaling a deep relaxing sigh. Then to Floss he said, "Just don't mind us."

Now it was Candy's turn to go on her girl. "Okay Juicey, I see you."

Floss knew all the lap dances had Buddy turned up. Hearing Juicey doing all that slurping and Candy fondling him, he got hard again. Before it was all over him and his boy got sucked up and even switched. Buddy had a video recorder in the car and each shared their turn holding it, while the girls taught step by step how to suck a dick.

The things bitches started doing just to be with a made man. All of it made it worth it to Floss.

***

Zeek was selling some property he owned. He took Floss to a nice 3-bedroom house in Reisterstown and asked him if he was interested in buying it.

"This snitchin' ass nigga red is putting me in a fucked up position," he explained. "So, I figure if I get convicted and have to do some time I'll have more than enough bread to take care of me, my girl and three kids."

Although Floss owned a home with Diddy, he did not own the one he stayed in with Tia and his son. "Let me holler at my girl and I'll let you know."

Tia was back on her bullshit. "I don't think we're ready," she said. Ever since he bought the benz and was back spending long nights out, their relationship turned ugly again.

"What do you mean?" he asked. "This is for you and my son. For our family."

Tossing her hands up Tia said, "Alright, whatever!" and walked out the bedroom. Floss got the house, giving Zeek $60,000 cash and from there took over the mortgage. He told Tia this would always be their home, so if something happened to him they would be alright.

Back in the streets, Floss did his best to stay low key by switching cars. He pushed Hertz rentals whenever he went to Freetown to see his boys. Whipping the Benz in those parts was asking for the police to pull him over, and things were too good.

Gary, from the dealership at the auto showcase, called him to come pick up the Escalade EXT he ordered. It was black on black sitting on 26" chrome rims. Floss shot right down there and fell in love with it, at first sight. Now, with two whips he put an order for a Lexus LS 430 ultra. He wanted this for Tia. Gary told him he would have it in a week.

All this splurging called for him to pick up the grind. Even though his investments with Diddy in property and the bail bondsman service was going good Floss wanted to accomplish his goal of getting out the game. So, gathering all the money, he met Zeek with $250,000. Being that this was going to be his last run and if everything went as planned.

"I wanna buy ten and I want you to front me ten," he said. "My plan is to break it all down. I'm not sellin' nothin' more than an ounce. I'm takin' it back to Freetown, on the block servin'."

Zeek was so thankful for all the support he got from Floss. "Man, i go chu. We come a long way. And I know you and I didn't see eye to eye at first, but I'm glad we clicked. Give me a few days and it's on."

Staying true to his word, Zeek looked out and like old times Floss found himself in tiffany's kitchen, in the projects, whipping the work with baking soda. But now instead of having only a few helping hands hustling the block, he had many. He was the new big don and being that this was going to be his last run he planned on leaving the game a millionaire. That was his dream.

CHAPTER TWENTY-ONE

Back at the federal holding facility ...... Present day.

After hearing how many business ventures he entered into Miles could not believe it. "Damn Floss, you were doin it big. How in the hell did you get caught up, if that was your last time coppin bricks from Zeek?"

"Well." he began. "About a week later I got a call from my uncle Smoke. He told me them people were following him. I mean the nigga was spooked! So, I believed him. Thank god too, because the next day I got pulled over by this Jeep Liberty."

Floss explained how the detectives that pulled him over and tore up his escalade EXT up. They called back-up and ran K-9's all over the truck. He didn't have any drugs or an excessive amount of money on him, so they were mad as hell they didn't find anything.

"They told me my friends weren't my friends. I didn't know what the fuck they meant by that, wondering who it was tellin on me. Then one of them said I was known to be the biggest drug dealer in Pasadena and my day was coming."

Miles shook his head. "Damn, that's crazy as fuck. What did you do next?"

"Shit, I stayed low key." he said. "But I still had to do my thing. So, I switched it up and stayed out of my Benz and truck. I parked the Q45 at T-Roy's grandmothers spot already so the only thing left to do was move in a rental. But that didn't last long either."

Floss told him how one day he was in a ford Taurus. He had a smoker rent it from the same hertz. He was at the light on Jumper's Whole Road and Baltimore Annapolis road when he saw the same Jeep Liberty in his rear view. When the light turned green, he punched the gas because he had 18 ounces rocked up on him. This led to a high-speed chase, but fortunately he lost them on some back roads.

"I jumped on interstate 100 and headed towards the 40." He continued to Miles. "When I got away something told me I was on borrowed time. So, I decided to use the home girl's tiffany and key to move the work to my other homeboys."

"I bet all this started around the time that nigga DC got popped, but you didn't know it." Miles said.

He was putting that together. "Yeah I know. All that time I thought this nigga was dead or something. From what my lawyer says, DC had been helping to bring down a few people."

"Whatever happened to Zeek?" his cellie asked next. "Did Red go through with tellin on him?"

Floss gave him a serious look. "Hell yeah! My boy got a life sentence last June."

"What happened to Red?"

"My boy told me Red hit the yard in Cumberland and two of the homies from Baltimore stabbed him up pretty bad."

"Did he die?"

"Nah, but his days are numbered." he said. "Zeek was loved and got people all over the system."

"Where he at now?"

"USP Hazelton. He and Big Don are on the same yard." Floss dropped his head.

"Those are two good men that lost their freedom by a snitch ass nigga."

That was how they ended their night. Thinking back on everything leading up to his arrest drained Floss to the point of exhaustion. When he laid down, he slept hard, dreaming of club parking lot shootings, Pyrex pots and crack heads walking like zombies up and down the block.

It was around 2am when he awoke. Flashes of a dream involving a high-speed chase with 100 police cars snatched his eyes open. When he looked around all he saw was the bunk, a dark cell and the window-slit cut out the concrete wall. Their only view to the outside world.

Leaning up on his elbow he looked out, and into the night's sky. The moon shined bright and he could not help but wonder what his father was doing at the same moment.

Was he looking out of a cell window also? He thought. Then Floss' attention drifted to his own son.

Damn.... How his dreams turned into nightmares. By the time the morning rolled around Floss got up to find Miles already moving about. After washing up and brushing his teeth he went to the phone and called T-Roy to see how his boy was making it.

"Wussup babyboy!" T-Roy's voice was full of life.

"Nothin much. What's good?"

"Same shit. Ole' girl candy asked about you. She said she wants to come up there and see you."

He laughed. "What the fuck Candy want?"

T-Roy was laughing also. "She said you're her boo! Me and the homie Rock slid up to Norma Jeans and all she kept talkin about was you and how the rest of these niggas is fakin."

"That's right." he said. "Tell her I said represent then. As far as visiting me, tell her Tia ain't havin that. Just let her know I'll be home soon."

"I will. So, what are they talkin' about?"

Floss explained how his court date was drawing near in two weeks. Then speaking in code, he smoothly asked about DC and if T-Roy was able to find someone at that jail.

"I'm still looking! But don't worry he will pop up."

Switching subjects, T-Roy told him how good his little brother and sister was doing and how his mom was driving a new whip. Floss didn't say nothing, but it was because of the money he had Diddy drop off from the house sell. "What's up with that nigga Boodah?" Floss asked next. "have you seen him?"

"I'm glad you said somethin'. He told me to have you call him. I got his number right here."

Floss jotted down the number.

"I think it's an emergency," T-Roy added. "He said make sure you hit him when you get it."

His curiosity got the best of him. "Alright cool. Let me hit him now then." hanging up Floss dialed Boodah's number. The phone rang twice before a female answered and accepted the collect call.

"Hello."

"Yes..umm, may I speak to Boodah?"

"Yes, he's right here," she said. Then in the background she said, "it's for you baby." Boodah's voice came deep over the line. "Yo, who's this?"

"It's Floss."

"Yo... My nigga.....what's up wit'chu?" came an excited Boodah.

"nothin.. Same shit you know. I just hit my man and he said you wanted me to call."

"I did. I did." Boodah's voice got calmer as he spoke. "Ayo, you remember ya boy they got up the way? The one you were trynah reach?"

He was talking about DC "Yea, what about him? You got his number?"

"Yeap, my boy do. He stays in the same apartment complex, two doors down from him."

Floss hearing Boodah had a homeboy who stayed in the same unit in the same Super Max jail, with DC was heaven sent. "Is that right?"

"No bullshit."

This was the best news he'd heard in weeks and it was right on time. "Look, I got somethin' proper for ya man if he gets that nigga's number."

But Boodah wasn't hearing it. "Man, what I tell you baby-boy? Don't disrespect me like that, I told you - I got you. Now chill out. I'll see you soon."

When Floss got off the phone he headed straight to his cell. Miles was making a cup of ramen soup in a cup when he walked in.

"Why you smilin' and shit?" his cellie asked.

"Man, you're not gonna believe this," he said rubbing his palms together. "I just got off the phone with Boodah. He has a homeboy who's in the unit with DC"

Miles was smiling too. "Oh yeah?"

He nodded. "Yep."

"Well shit, what did he say? Is he gonna repay you for the favor and smash that nigga?" Miles asked.

"Yea, he told me not to worry. He would handle it." Floss was happy as hell. "With DC out of the way, the government wouldn't have a case and they would have to let me go. He's the last informant."

***

Days passed and when the weekend rolled around Floss got a visit from Tia and his mother. His demeanor made his mother ask why he was smiling so much, and he simply told her he knew he was coming home. He was so glad he bought the house for Tia and his son. Now at least he'd have his own spot to go to when he got out. "Your dad sends his love," his mom told him.

"How's he doin?"

"Fine."

"How about you?" he asked next. "I heard you're around flaunting in your new whip." She smiled. "Boy I don't flaunt nothing around."

But Tia disagreed. "She lyin'. You should see how she be leanin' in that beamer. Now I see where you be getting' it from."

Floss started laughing. "Like that huh?"

His mother just shrugged her shoulders. "Some habits are hard to get rid of."

It had been a long time since he had a visit that wasn't sad and gloomy. Tia didn't bring his son, who was at her mother's house in Baltimore. So, they took this time to talk about him back to live with them.

"It's time to leave them streets alone," his mother said agreeing with Tia. "After this is behind you and you come home, just remember what it almost cost you."

"I am Ma."

Tia was glad. "Is love you and as long as you're trying to be the man i need you to be then I'll always take you back."

That's all he wanted to hear.

When he got back to the unit Floss jumped right on the phone. He wanted to call T-Roy because he needed him to pick up some money from Diddy. Staying true as a friend and business partner Diddy was still grinding with the bail bonds service. Floss was a silent partner the whole time, so he was still drawing interest from all profit. "Wussup nigga!" T-Roy answered on the first ring.

Leaning against the wall Floss said, "Nothin much. Aye, hit Diddy up. He got some bread for me. I need you to drop it off at my mom's."

"Cool I got chu. Did you get at that nigga Boodah yet?"

"Yea, I called him."

"What did he want?"

Choosing his words correctly he said. "He found the nigga who use to be down with the horsemen."

"Oh yea? So that's good news, right?"

"Yep."

"So, what now?"

"We just wait," he said. T-Roy didn't want to ask any more questions, so he switched the subject. He told Floss how the police task force was conducting raids in Freetown and how tiffany was locked up. She got popped with 18 ounces rocked up and a Glock 9mm. 'The feds picked it up" T-Roy said.

"Damn." Floss was fucked up about it. All the stuff she did to help him this was the last thing he wanted to hear. "Look, take two hundred out of that money Diddy gives you and make sure it gets on her books."

"I will. And listen, don't worry. You'll be back soon. So just chill."

Floss got off the phone and his positive vibe turned somber. He hated hearing anyone getting busted for trying to survive and provide for their children. Tiffany helped everyone and he knew that despite being a young, black, single mother she did it for her son. She wasn't on welfare or nothing. But now she was locked up and there was no telling where her son was.

At that moment, he realized how treacherous the game really was. He promised himself he was done with it completely. The only thing he needed now was for his trial to be canceled so he could go home.

All he wanted was to get out and be there for his son.

CHAPTER TWENTY-TWO

I t was 10 days before his trial date and Floss was still waiting on word about DC. He didn't want to call Boodah
back because of the phones being recorded. He would
just have to trust the guy's word. In the meantime, it was
Miles who was stressing a lot. Turning down his own plea,
Miles was facing a bunch of time if he lost in trial as well.

"Inmate Jefferson! Inmate Jefferson! Miles Jefferson!"
The C.O. called out from the front door.

Floss was on the phone talking to Tia when he heard his
cellie's name being called. He looked towards the cell and saw
Miles step out.

"Wussup?" he answered.

The C.O. said, "Roll it up. You're being moved to
another unit."

Tossing his hands in the air Miles got upset. "What?
Man, why ya'll moving me?"

Now it was the officer's turn to get upset. "You don't ask
the questions. Get your shit and let's go!" Not sure what the
problem was Floss told Tia he'd call her back, then he went
to the cell.

"Man, this is some bullshit!" Miles was pissed the hell
off as he packed his stuff.

"Why they movin' you?" Floss asked when he stepped in the cell.

"I don't know."

The officer came to the cell door. "Are you ready?" Floss asked, "What they moving him for?"

The CO was an older white guy who was strict as hell. But he seemed to relax a bit.

"I don't know. I just got the call to move him to the hole."

"The hole!" both he and Miles said in unison.

Miles was really confused now. "For what? I haven't done shit."

The officer said, "I think it's your case. Is it a violent charge?"

"Yea, but there a lot of violent people in this unit."

Shrugging his shoulders, the CO said, "Listen, they may feel like... Since you're probably facing a lot of time, maybe you would react violently if you're convicted. I've seen them do that to people, putting them in the hole."

The whole situation was messed up and Floss knew his cellie didn't want to be in the hole. Miles was stressing too much and not having someone to talk to, to help him through it, could cause him to act out violently. But there was nothing either of them could do about it.

Miles packed his belongings with a depressed look on his face. When he finished Floss pulled up on him and gave him some dap and a half a hug. "Look man," he said to his cellie. "You're going to be alright."

"I know," Miles said shaking his head. "But the hole? Damn, they could've just left me here. I'll be cool."

"Me and you know that. But it's just precaution. You know some of these niggas can't take their time and come back trippin', committing suicide and shit."

Miles laughed. "I guess you're right."

The CO added. "Yea, after you're sentenced they should put you back in general population;"

Helping Miles feel better, the man shouldered his personal items and bed roll. "Well man," he began. "I wish you luck as well. Don't trip, you'll be back on the streets in no time."

Floss smiled. "Thanks man." Then he looked at the CO. "Since ya'll takin my cellie, I'm lettin' ya'll know now, I'm not taking another cat in the cell with me."

The officer raised his hands in submission. "Hey, I don't run the place. I just unlock doors and escort inmates where they tell me to. That's all."

Miles laughed and said to Floss, "Ayo, don't buck on'em. Don't buck." he laughed. "It was cool meeting you baby-boy. We'll get back."

Floss gave him a head nod and smile. "Fa sho."

Seeing Miles leave like that was fucked up to him. After spending so much time together in a cell, helping each other through tough times with their cases, Floss got close to Miles. But life was like that and despite being locked up they both had their own separate paths to walk in life.

Floss had the cell to himself now so he was cool. Nobody dared asked him to move in, knowing he didn't fuck with many people anyway. He spent his days talking on the phone and working out and his nights reading. Although his trial date was approaching very fast he wasn't worried one bit.

Finally, the word came when he called T-Roy . It was 1 week exactly from his trial date "Call Boodah."

"Cool. Let me hit you back then," was all he said.

Disconnecting he dialed boodan's home number, hoping to catch him there. His girl answered on the second ring and accepted the call.

"Hello." came her sweet voice over the phone.

"Hey, is Boodah there?"

She said, "No Floss. But he told me to tell you he paid that bill for you. So don't worry about it. You hear me? Don't worry, it's paid."

"Okay," he replied. "Tell him thank you. My mom won't have to worry no more."

"No, she won't."

After saying goodbye, Floss hung up. An overwhelming sensation filled his soul to know that dc was out of the equation. That meant he now had no snitches testifying against him. There was no one to support the government's claims against him.

Damn, he thought smiling to himself as he took a seat in the dayroom.

A few guys were hanging out watching TV and playing cards. This older black dude from Baltimore took a seat across from him, nursing a cup of black coffee. Floss spoke to him every now and again because he reminded him of his pops.

"Aye OG, what's up?"

The man sipped the cup. "Nothing youngsta. I see they got'cho cellie."

He nodded. "yea, but I'll be cool."

"Ain't chu going to trial soon?"

"Next week."

"How's it lookin'?"

He shrugged. "Good on my end. I feel confident the government can't beat me in trial." "Well, sounds like you lookin' good."

"Yea, all I need now is to holler at my lawyer. I'm prayin he....."

On cue, the officer on the loudspeaker called his name.

"Inmate Blacksmith you got a lawyer visit."

Old school said, "Damn boy, ya need to pray for some big booty stripper bitches to come see us next."

Floss got up from the table. "Forreal huh? Damn...."

Heading to his cell he put on his Nike tennis shoes and then went to the door. Inside he hoped his lawyer was going to tell him he was going home right then.

Mr. Ravenall looked at him from across the table. His eyes were wide as he emphasized his point.

"I'm off your case! Plain and simple!"

"Man, how in the fuck...they can't do that. I paid you all that money." Floss couldn't believe his ears. His lawyers saying the court removed him from representing him was insane.

At the mentioning of money Mr. Ravenall said, "Well it's included in the premium package you bought for my representation that if I'm removed from your case by judicial ruling, I am not obligated to refund my fees."

The only thing Floss heard was no refund. "What!" he shook his head, confused. "Listen," the lawyer began. "The US attorney is making claims that I'm feeding you information, which is indirectly bringing death to those informants. I'm lucky they're not trying to indict me."

"But we ain't have nothing to do with them dudes dying," Floss said. "We can't control what the streets do. That's a consequence they choose when they decided to snitch." Mr. Ravenall nodded his head but still he had no other choice. "Listen, as of right now I'm off your case and it doesn't look like I'll be back on."

He shrugged and asked, "So who's my attorney now?"

"Honestly, I don't know. But who cares? The government has no informant. They can give you a public defender. There won't be a trial."

That's what he wanted to hear. "Okay, so how is this gonna play out? At least tell me that, before you leave me hangin'."

The lawyer explained that his last meeting with the US attorney prosecuting him was pissed the hell off and asked if he was willing to cop to a deal. When told he didn't think so the government showed signs of weakness. Mr. Ravenall told Floss he saw him getting the charges dismissed before trial or at worst called to a court date only to be offered a deal.

"What if I don't take it?"

"Then they will have to drop all charges sooner than later."

Floss stood and shook the lawyer's hand. "Well that's what I wanna hear. I appreciate all the things you did for me anyway."

Mr. Ravenall stood as well. "Honestly, I felt like I could beat the charges against you. But regardless how it played out with those guys, I'm glad you will be back on the streets. I need more paying customers out there."

Laughing he said, "Shit, you don't have to worry about me no more. The game is fucked up with all this snitchin' shit."

The man winked. "Keep my number just in case because you never know."

That night, laying on his bunk, Floss thought back over this entire experience. He never in a million years thought that things would unfold like this. Him being caught up in something that only murder could solve. Events that dated back to him at 17 years old with T-Roy, Rock, and DC. How old beefs with a cat like Boodah, something bringing them together later and down the line, behind a common cause. How they had to come to the feds to get some understanding of each other.

The game had been good to him. As he laid there Floss remembered the streets, and all that awaited him. He didn't know how but he would have to finally say goodbye to his old life. Candy, Juicey, and all his other side chicks would have to take a hike. Tia was all he was concerned about now. There was no way he'd get out and do her bad after she stayed down like that, there was no way.

He had taken her through too much.

***

The night the police finally got him Floss had just left the house with Tia. They had been arguing and he was staying wherever he laid his head. But like always they agreed to meet up and ended up having the best sex ever.

When he woke it was bright and early. He had finished paying the balance on the 20 bricks to Zeek and was finally done with the game. He felt this would be a good time to take a vacation.

After telling Tia he needed to go to the bails bondsman company to drop off some money to Diddy, he promised to come back ASAP. He hopped in his Benz and no sooner than he got to the turning lane of Marley Neck and Baltimore Annapolis Road intersection, he noticed the Jeep Liberty and two more unmarked cars following him. At first he thrught he was being paranoid. But when the flashing blue and red lights hit him he knew it was real.

That was his last day free. They confiscated $327,000 in cash and took him downtown to Northern District police station. He was told if he agreed to snitch they would let him go. If not, he was going to be detained.

"Fuck yall! Call my lawyer!" he barked.

He was taken downtown to east 101 Lombard Street. There the feds picked up the case. After 3 months he was transferred to Talbert county jail, where he continued to sit awaiting trial.

Now...folding his hands behind his head, Floss exhaled a long breath. It had been over 10 months since he left Tia in that bed. Smiling to himself in the dark he knew that in one week he'd be back, finally.

"You stayed real," he said to himself. "And never broke. Big Don would be proud." with that he closed his eyes fantasizing about all the stripper pussy he wouldn't be getting when he got out.

Nah.... He was finally a one woman's man.

CHAPTER TWENTY-THREE

Three days before his trial was to start, Floss found out Diddy was being indicted on multiple charges from money laundering to conspiracy to distribute more than 5 kilos of cocaine. The feds had stormed his home and business, confiscating legal documents and over $198,000 in cash.

Already concerned, Floss was hoping for his own charges to be dismissed. Tia came and relayed all the breaking news. He sent her to visit Diddy, who was being held at bccc. His main concern was if his name was being linked to Diddy's case.

"He says as of now, he doesn't know," she said, "They still haven't given you a lawyer yet?"

He shook his head. "nah and I'm hoping they're not gonna have to."

"Well don't stress bae. Everything gonna be alright," she said encouraging him. "Diddy should have shut shit down when you got arrested. But he didn't pay attention to the signs."

He had heard Diddy was doing some major stunting since he had been gone. "Yea, you're probably right. I haven't gotten any notices of indictment, so I should be cool." Floss' positive attitude carried him on. The next day he was called to a lawyer's visit and all that positivity disappeared. He went to the small conference room anticipating the worst. What he met was a short fat white man in his 50's with gold wire rimmed glasses.

"Hello Mr. Blacksmith, I'm Mr. Thompson." The man was smiling with his hand extended. "I'll be representing you at trial."

Floss shook his hand. "Nice to meet you." The mentioning of trial made him pause.

"So, I will be going trial?"

They sat opposite of each other. The desk between them held manila folders which Mr. Thompson opened. "Well after looking at your case it seems the government really has no evidence or witnesses." the two men locked eyes at the word witnesses.

The lawyer continued, "I'm well acquainted with your last lawyer, Mr. Ravenall and he forwarded me all his paperwork. After talking to the US attorney, I'm inclined to believe your trial date will be a turnaround."

He didn't understand. "A turnaround? What does that mean?"

"It means, the marshals will bring you to your scheduled court date and bring you back here," he explained. "In other words, I have the government dismissing the charges for lack of evidence."

Hearing the words numbed him. But he didn't want to get his hopes up. "Well why have the court date at all then?"

"Because dismissing charges isn't something the government does lightly. They'll wait until the last minute, praying something occurs in their favor."

With that said he thought about Diddy's case. "Are you aware of anything that might or could probably happen against me?"

The lawyer shook his head. "Nope. You have no other charges pending and no - witnesses testifying against you. Unless the devil himself pops up the morning of... Mr. Blacksmith you'll be a free man."

Floss was now smiling from ear to ear. "Well, that's what I wanna hear."

"I figured so," the lawyer said standing. "I just wanted to come down and meet you, as well as give you an update. I know you've been in the blind, so now you can tell your family not to worry."

Thanks man. And even though you are court appointed, let me know how much you charge, and I'll handle that."

The man waved it off. "It's nothing really. How can I charge you for a turnaround?"

But Floss felt the turnaround was priceless. "Man, if I get turned around you can name your price."

The two of them shared a good laugh.

***

The morning of his trial date Floss was awakened around 4 a.m. His cell was unlocked 30 minutes later, and he enjoyed an apple and milk for breakfast. He and 5 other inmates were going to court that morning and he was praying he wouldn't be returning with them.

After sitting in a holding cell for a few hours, Floss and the others were chained by marshals and taken to the downtown federal courthouse. There they were shackled and placed in another holding cell.

One cat with them was a young hustler from Annapolis named Pistol. Floss had heard he was at the jail on a few charges, but never seen him. Pistol was one of the main shooters helping to fight for Boodah's cause when all the beef was popping off. Now that things were different between them Pistol saw Floss in another light.

Giving Floss some dap Pistol said, "What's up? You cool?"

He nodded. "Yea. How about you?"

The man said, "Shit, as cool as a nigga can be, about to sign for 327 months."

The 27 years Pistol spoke of made Floss say, "Damn baby boy, that's the deal?"

He nodded. "Yep. It's either that or a lot more." Pistol was being held for five bank

robberies, multiple gun charges and two car jackings. "At least I'll have a date. I'm only 22 so I'll be out by forty-seven."

Floss was still shaking his head.

"What about you?" he asked. "How's your shit lookin'? The streets saying you should be good to get out."

"It's lookin' like that. My new lawyer says this should be a turnaround. So I'm just here for the ride."

"That's good." pistol gave him some dap. "You know... I tip my hat to you for what - you did for Boodah. Anything I can do, let me know. I know we had our issues in the past but real recognize real."

Floss respected and appreciated the gesture. "Thanks man. You just keep your head up.

When I get out, I'll holler at Boodah, so we can put something together for you." One of the marshals came and started calling out names.

"Anderson..... Jackson....Davis..... Hernandez...."

A white dude, a mexican, pistol, and another black guy all stepped to the front. Pistol said, "Well I'll be back in a minute."

Floss wished him well and took a seat on the bench.

***

Two hours passed and lunch was served. Floss wasn't hungry. He just wanted to finish his day and return to the jail so he could be released. When the marshals called his name and told him he had a lawyer visit he got up and stepped to the front. He figured Mr. Thompson was there to give him an update. Hopefully, he wouldn't have to step foot in a court room.

The marshal led him to a small room. Mr. Thompson was seated at a table. When he entered the man stood and the marshal left out closing the door behind him.

"How's it going?"

Floss shrugged. "Cool. You tell me? I'm ready to leave this hell hole."

Exhaling a long sigh Mr. Thompson said, "Well that may well happen, but not today." "What? Why not?" He couldn't believe his ears.

"They're talking about beginning trial." Floss was confused. "Trial? How? They have no informants."

The lawyer removed his wire-rimmed glasses and said, "It seems they do. Just this morning I got a call from their office saying they have someone who has stepped in and is willing to testify against you."

He couldn't believe his ears. "Testify? For what?"

Mr. Thompson turned the pages on the tablet before him. "Conspiracy to commit murder, murder, conspiracy to distribute ten kilograms of cocaine, money laundering, tampering with a governmental witness..."

Floss cut him off. "Tampering with... Man what the fuck are you talking about? Who in the hell is their witness?"

"I don't know," the lawyer said confused himself. "But they're serious. I even asked if there was possibly a deal on the table."

"I'm not taking no bitch ass deals!" he barked.

Mr. Thompson said, "And they're not offering any. Which lets me know whoever they got; they feel is reliable."

Floss was lost for words. "So, what does this mean? What are we gonna do?"

The lawyer looked at his watch and said, "Well trial is set to begin. I just wanted to prepare you for what's to come."

"Prepare me? Man, we haven't even had a single discussion about the case." Floss was livid. "Can you ask for it to be pushed back?"

"I plan to. In the meantime, just relax. Whoever it is they got testifying, if we're granted a continuance, I'm sure we can find a way to discredit their claims against you."

Floss was taken back to the holding cell. His whole world had been turned completely upside down. He sat there on the bench in a daze. Fifteen minutes after his lawyer visit, he was called again. But this time he was taken to a courtroom and seated next to his lawyer, at a small table. A white man sat at the table next to them and he knew this guy was the government.

"All rise for the honourable Samuel Wright."

As the bailiff called the court to stand an old white judge entered the room. Floss looked around and saw his mother, Tia, his son, and grandma seated in the audience. The judge took his seat and on cue his lawyer stood.

"Your Honor, I ask for a continuance. I was just appointed to this case and have not been fully prepared to represent my client." Mr. Thompson said addressing the court.

The government objected. "Your Honor, this matter has been on the docket for ten months already. Counsel has been fully informed by my office and the previous Attorney who was representing the defendant."

The judge said, "Continuance is denied. I call this matter, US vs. Blacksmith to come to order."

Floss began looking around the courtroom. His eyes locked on his mother and Tia. They were smiling. Deep inside he began to feel better. But as the trial began, he became unsure.

He leaned over to whisper to his lawyer. "Where they witness?"

Mr. Thompson said, "I'm not sure. Maybe..."

The sound of a door opening, and chains rattling drew their attention to the side of the courtroom. Out of a backroom a deputy exited followed by someone dressed in an orange jumpsuit.

"What the...."

When Floss first saw Miles, he couldn't believe his eyes. But when the deputy escorted him to the chair on the stand, he knew his whole world was turning upside down.

Miles dropped his eyes unable to look at him.

"Do you know him?" his lawyer asked.

Shaking his head Floss said, "Yea. He was my cellie in the county jail."

Mr. Thompson shook his head and said, "Fuck me. I can't believe this shit. Don't tell me you told him anything that could incriminate you."

Floss looked at the man and simply said, "I told him everything."

His lawyer wiped his forehead. There was nothing he could say. With no deal on the - table he knew that this trial was over before it began. There was no way he could win a fight when his client had given all the bullets to the man firing the gun at him. There was no way.

For 3 hours Floss sat in the courtroom that day listening to Miles debrief everything he told to him. But the crushing blow came when the government played a tape recorder of him confessing to killing los and plotting the murder of his own informants. Miles admitted to wearing a wire in the cell on numerous occasions. No matter how aggressive his lawyer tried to attack mile's claims, Floss knew his odds weren't good. And when he turned and looked at his family, he found them in tears.

"So, he admitted to murders, laundering money, selling drugs and witness tampering," the prosecutor said. "Is there anything else?"

Miles thought for a moment and said, "Nah... Nothing I can think of right now."

"And for this information were you promised anything? I mean, as a reward for your testimony?"

"I wasn't promised anything," he said. "Only that it may help me in my own case."

"But not promised am I correct?"

Floss jumped out of his seat. "You snitch ass bitch! I'll kill you," he screamed out loud. The judge banged the gavel. "Order in the court! Order in the court!" Miles was wide eyed with fear.

"I'll kill you, your mom, and your whole family you bitch!" Floss promised Miles. He heard his mother cry out.

Bang! Bang!

The judge hammered the gavel. "Bailiff remove him from my courtroom now!"

Floss was hysterical. He lost all sight of reality. He didn't see or hear his mother and Tia calling his name. All he saw was red. He wanted to kill Miles and every snitch in the world. With two deputies grabbing and wrestling him out of the courtroom, he fought against their restraints. His dreams had turned to a nightmare and the devil himself was his own cellie who appeared the morning of trial.

EPILOGUE

3 days later........

T he cell was dark and cold. Floss hadn't left out to do a single thing. He hadn't eaten, showered and barely got up to use the bathroom. Since blowing trial he had become numb to everything around him. It was like all of life had stood still, and he couldn't breathe. Now, as he laid on the thin mat beneath a wool blanket, he began to shed tears.

Money laundering.

Conspiracy to commit murder.

Conspiracy to distribute 50 kilos or more.

All equaling a life sentence.

Never in a million years had he thought this would happen. He couldn't believe he could be so green as to sit there and let Miles plot on him like that. Someone who played the part to the tee, only to slither up under him.

Immediately after being removed from the courtroom, Floss was taken to a holding cell. His lawyer Mr. Thompson came to see him, asking him to pull it together for his mother and Tia. It took 20-minutes after being told Miles was no longer in the courtroom. Then he was escorted back where the jury found him guilty on all counts.

The judge set sentencing two weeks away, so all Floss could thing about was KC and Joe-Joe's song called Life. At his lawyer visit, the next day, Mr. Thompson told him he would more than likely get life, but they would appeal.

Facing Tia was the hardest. The next day she came to visit him, despite him asking her not to come. Of course, she wasn't having that. She had to see him alone, so she left his son at home.

"Remember our first night?" she asked him.

Floss thought back to when they first met.

When him, T-Roy and her girl all went to the motel. How he had taken her virginity which hooked him ever since.

"Yeah," he said. His eyes were puffy from not getting any sleep that night.

Tia took a real good look at him. "I was so scared," she told him. "You were my first.

But when you promised not to hurt me, and that it would be okay, I believed you."

Floss saw the tears in her eyes.

Tia leaned in closer and put her hand up to the Plexiglas. "Baby, I promise you.... I got 'chu and it's gonna be alright."

Floss put his hand up to hers and nodded his head, holding his composure. "I know bae, I know. I just need for you to stay strong for me."

She nodded. "And you for me...

Her words echoed in his mind as he laid there, in his cell. He was oblivious to the sounds being made outside his door in the unit. The card games, dominos, and tv watchers. All of them were non-existent to him.

That's when he heard his name called over the loudspeaker.

"Inmate Blacksmith ...lawyer visit! Report to the slider for your visit!"

At first, he simply laid there. He thought he was hearing things since Mr. Thompson had just came to see him the day before.

Floss jumped up. "Man, what the fuck?"

He was in a bad mood. His mind immediately jumped to the thought that Mr. Thompson's re-emergence concerned an appeal fee. He knew the man wanted to milk him out of some of the money he had.

Jumping up, Floss put on his orange suit and before going to the slider, an officer came and escorted him to the lawyer visit. Mr. Thompson hadn't arrived yet, so the officer put him inside the room and left him there.

Instantly he began thinking about escaping. His eyes began looking at the ceiling, trying to figure out if he saw a way out. Just as his mind began racing a door opened and in came Mr. Thompson.

"Aye Floss," the man said referring to him by his street name for the first time.

Floss hadn't noticed, he was still looking around. "Ayo, where does the ceiling lead too?" he asked.

"Huh?" The lawyer asked as he moved all jittery. He took a seat across from Floss. "What kind of question is that?"

Finally, Floss looked up and saw Mr. Thompson. The man's hair was tossed in a stringy mess, there was a white powdery substance on his left nostril, and he looked high as a kite. "Man, I'm thinking about options to getting out of here."

"Like escape?"

Floss quickly silenced him. "Sshh!" he said putting his finger to his lips. Then lowering his voice, he said, "Man, is you high? Cause you geekin' like shit. Wipe your nose, you got shit on it."

Mr. Thompson's face twitched, and he fidgeted with his gold rim glasses before wiping his nose off. "I had a long night. But to answer your question that ceiling leads to the officer's lounge."

Disappointment spread across Floss's face fast. Then he grew upset again. "Why the fuck is you up here, high and shit?" For the man to think this was a game, and to see his counsel in this rare state made Floss feel like he's been set up.

But the man said, "I came because I have some good news." Floss was caught off guard.

Mr. Thompson continued, "The judge sent emails out this morning ordering a mistrial, and ordering for a new one to begin in 60-days."

"A mistrial?" He was confused.

"Yeah, so... He ruled that the government's star witness, who was your cellmate, his testimony was not credible."

Floss looked at the man. "But what about the tape recorder?" He said. "Miles wore a wire on me."

Mr. Thompson acted like he missed Floss's admission of guilt. "The government had no expert to validate that was in fact your voice on the tape. You might've missed when I objected to its use on the fact."

He did miss that. "So, what does this all mean?"

"It means we start all over from scratch," the man said. "As of right now you have no sentence. It's just like when you first got arrested.

His heart raced with hope. "So, there's no sentencing in two weeks?"

"Nope, "Mr. Thompson said standing up. "Now, I gotta go. I came as fast as I could to tell you. And Floss, excuse my presence. Despite what you may think, I know the law. Plus, we still have Ravenell. So, at the end of the day, you have a good legal team willing to do whatever."

Floss had no idea this turn of event would come into his life. Never in a million years. Hearing he was granted a new trial meant he still had hope. But as long as Miles was still around....or anyone else who felt the need to jump on his case....he would always be in danger.

Which meant, he had to fight.

That night when he laid down, there were no tears. Only plans. There was no way he was going to see Miles coming and let him win the war. Miles had violated and now he had to pay the cost.

THE END

www.ingramcontent.com/pod-product-compliance
Lightning Source LLC
Chambersburg PA
CBHW021157010426
R18062100001B/R180621PG41931CBX00003B/3

* 9 7 8 0 9 9 6 6 2 5 2 4 1 *